New Country Sampler

Crafts, Decorating, and Stenciling

Publications International, Ltd.

Contributing Craft Designers:
Gerry Bauman/The Farmhouse (page 118); Lori Blankenship (pages 36, 73); Sue Carson (pages 137, 162); Pam Cowley (page 140); Walter B. Fedyshyn, AIFD, PFCI (pages 24, 86); Ricë Freeman-Zachery (page 68); Judy Gibbs/Hollie Designs (pages 46, 48, 58, 103, 167); Janelle Hayes (pages 115, 146, 172); Trena Hegdahl (page 43); Allan Howze (page 120); Janet Immordino (pages 20, 22, 32, 34, 60, 76, 98, 106, 130, 160, 170); Charlene Messerle (pages 108, 112, 122); Carol Neu (pages 78, 83, 134, 152, 155); Jan Patek/Jan Patek Quilts (page 148); The Robins & Willoughby Collection at L.A. Stencilworks (pages 23, 33, 61, 90, 184, 192, 200, 208, 228, 250); Abby Ruoff (pages 96, 132, 144); Judith Sandstrom (page 100); Vicki Schweitzer (pages 53, 62, 70, 80, 88); Ann Snuggs (page 110); Muriel Spencer (page 124); Karen Almy Stovall (page 38); Nancy Tribolet/Stencils by Nancy (pages 21, 25, 35, 77, 196, 204, 216, 224, 232, 236, 241, 246); Dee Dee Triplett (pages 29, 92); Leanne Watson/Primitive Designs (pages 51, 188, 212, 220); Kathy Wirth (pages 18, 26, 40, 50).

Contributing Photography: PDR Productions, Inc.; Sacco Productions Limited/Chicago, IL; Silver Lining Digital, Inc.

Decorative Border Art: The Robins & Willoughby Collection at L.A. Stencilworks (pages 18–94, 184–253); Leanne Watson/Primitive Designs (pages 96–174).

Manufactured in China.

8 7 6 5 4 3 2 1

ISBN: 1-4127-1043-X

Library of Congress Control Number: 2004102746

Contents

Craft Techniques

Create the genuine warmth of a country home

by crafting with your own handmade touch!

What is more country than crafting? Nothing! You can make the wonderful projects in these books as gifts, for yourself, or add them to your home decor. Many of the projects take a day or less to create. Once you begin, you'll see that creating your own gifts and decorations is a satisfying and relaxing way to spend your free time.

Take a moment to look through these pages. You'll find everything from counted cross-stitch to decorative wood painting. Each project has complete step-by-step instructions and photos to help make everything easy to understand and fun to do. There are projects for all skill levels and interests.

After familiarizing yourself with these basic techniques and flipping through the pages, it's time to choose your first project. Remember, things made by hand come from the heart. So have fun creating these wonderful crafts and decorations.

A Word About Glue

Glue can be a sticky subject when you don't use the right one for the job. There are many different glues on the craft market today, each formulated for a different crafting purpose. The following are ones you should be familiar with:

CRAFT GLUE This may be used as an all-purpose glue—it dries clear and flexible. It is often referred to as white glue or tacky glue. Tacky on contact, it allows you to put two items together without a lot of set-up time required. Use it for most projects, especially ones involving wood, plastics, some fabrics, and cardboard.

FABRIC GLUE This type of glue is made to bond with fabric fibers and withstand repeated washing. Use this glue for attaching rhinestones and/or other charms to fabric projects. Some glues require heat-setting. Check the bottle for complete instructions.

LOW-MELT GLUE This is similar to hot-melt glue in that it is formed into sticks and requires a glue gun to be used. Low-melt glue is used for projects that would be damaged by heat, such as foam, balloons, and metallic ribbons. Low-melt glue sticks are oval-shaped and can only be used in a low-temperature glue gun.

HOT-MELT GLUE Formed into cylindrical sticks, this glue is inserted into a hot-temperature glue gun and heated to a liquid state. Depending on the type of glue gun used, the glue is forced out through the gun's nozzle by either pushing on the end of the glue stick or squeezing a trigger. Use clear glue sticks for projects using wood, fabrics, most plastics, ceramics, and cardboard. When using any glue gun, be careful of the nozzle and the freshly applied glue—it is very hot! Apply glue to the piece being attached. Work with small areas so the glue doesn't set before objects are pressed into place.

THIN-BODIED GLUES Use these glues when your project requires a smooth, thin layer of glue. Thin-bodied glues work well on some fabrics and papers.

General Pattern Instructions

ENLARGING PATTERNS Many of the patterns in this book are printed smaller than actual size in order to fit them on the page. You will have to enlarge them before using them. You can do this on a photocopier, copying the pattern at the percentage indicated.

CUTTING OUT PATTERNS When a project's instructions tell you to cut out a shape according to the pattern, trace the pattern from the book onto tracing paper, using a pencil. If the pattern has an arrow with the word FOLD next to a line, it is a half pattern. Fold a sheet of tracing paper in half, and open up the paper. Place the fold line of the tracing paper exactly on top of the fold line of the pattern, and trace the pattern with a pencil. Then refold, and cut along the line, going through both layers. Open paper for the full pattern.

For transferring patterns onto objects, see page 10 of the Decorative Wood Painting section.

Cross-Stitch

Cross-stitch is traditionally worked on an "even-weave" cloth that has vertical and horizontal threads of equal thickness and spacing. Six-strand embroidery floss is used for most stitching; there are also many beautiful threads that can be used to enhance the appearance of the stitching.

Basic Supplies

FABRIC The most common even-weave fabric is 14-count Aida cloth. The weave of this fabric creates distinct squares that make stitching very easy for beginning or novice cross-stitchers.

FLOSS Six-strand cotton embroidery floss is most commonly used, and it's usually cut into 18-inch lengths for stitching. Use two of the six strands for stitching on 14-count Aida cloth. Also use two strands for backstitching.

NEEDLES, HOOPS, AND SCISSORS

A blunt-end or tapestry needle is used for counted cross-stitch. A #24 needle is the recommended size for stitching on 14-count Aida cloth. You may use an embroidery hoop while stitching—just be sure to remove it when not working on the project. A small pair of sharp scissors are a definite help when working with embroidery floss.

Preparing to Stitch

To locate the center of the cloth, lightly fold the fabric in half and in half again. Find the center of the chart by following the arrows on the sides. Begin stitching here and work outward.

Each square on the chart equals one stitch on the fabric. The colors correspond to the floss numbers listed in the color key. Select a color, and stitch all of that color within an area. Hold the thread ends behind the fabric

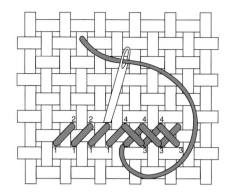

Figure A

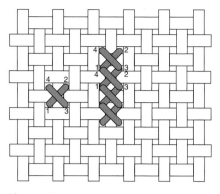

Figure B

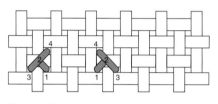

Figure C

until secured or covered over with two or three stitches. You may skip a few stitches on the back of the material, but do not run the thread from one area to another behind a section that will not be stitched in the finished piece—it will show through the fabric. If your thread begins to twist, drop the needle and allow the thread to untwist. Keep an even tension when pulling stitches through so that all stitches have a uniform look. To end a thread, weave or run the thread under several stitches on the back.

Each counted cross-stitch is represented by a colored square on the project's chart. For horizontal rows, work the stitches in two steps, i.e., all of the left to right stitches and then all of the right to left stitches (see Figure A). For vertical rows, work each complete stitch as shown in Figure B. Three-quarter stitches are often used when the design requires two

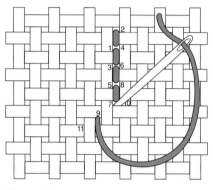

Figure D

colors in one square or to allow more detail in the pattern (see Figure C). The backstitch is often used to outline or create letters and is shown by bold lines on the patterns. Backstitch is usually worked after the pattern is completed (see Figure D).

Plastic Canvas

Plastic canvas allows for three-dimensional stitchery projects to be constructed. Plastic canvas is easy to do, easy on the eyes, and easy on the pocketbook, too.

Basic Supplies

PLASTIC CANVAS Canvas is most widely available by the sheet. Stitch all the pieces of a project on the same brand of plastic canvas to ensure that the meshes will match when you join them together. Plastic canvas comes in several counts or mesh sizes (number of stitches per inch) and numerous sizes of sheets. Specialty sizes and shapes such as circles are also available. Most canvas is clear, although up to 24 colors are available. Colored canvas is used when parts of the project remain unstitched. Seven-count canvas comes in four weights: standard, flexible, stiff, and soft (made especially for bending and curved projects). Designs can be stitched on any mesh count—the resulting size of the project is the only thing that will be affected. The smaller the count number, the larger the project will be.

NEEDLE Needle size is determined by the count size of the plastic canvas you are using. Patterns generally call for a #18 needle for stitching on 7-count canvas, a #16 or #18 for 10-count canvas, and a #22 or #24 for stitching on 14-count canvas.

YARNS A wide variety of yarns may be used. The most common is worsted weight (or four-ply). Acrylic yarns are less expensive and are washable; wool may also be used. Several companies produce specialty yarns for plastic canvas work. These cover the canvas well and will not "pill" as some acrylics do. Sport weight yarns (or three-ply) and embroidery floss are often used on 10-count canvas. Use 12 strands or double the floss thickness for 10-count canvas and 6 strands for stitching on 14-count canvas. On

14-count canvas, many of the specialty metallic threads made for cross-stitch can be used to highlight and enhance your project.

Cutting Out Your Project

Many plastic canvas projects are dimensional—a shape has to be cut out and stitched. Scissors or a craft knife are recommended.

Preparing to Stitch

Cut your yarn to a 36-inch length. Begin by holding the yarn end behind the canvas until secured or covered over with two or three stitches. To end a length, weave or run the yarn under several stitches on the back. Cut the end close to the canvas. The continental stitch is the most commonly used stitch. Decorative stitches will add interest and texture to your project. As in cross-stitch, if your yarn begins to twist, drop the needle and allow the yarn to untwist. Do not pull stitches too tightly; this will cause gaps in the stitching and allow canvas to show. Also, do not carry one color yarn across too many rows of another color on the back—the carried color may show through to the front. Do not stitch the outer edge of the canvas until the other stitching is complete. If the project is a single piece of canvas, overcast the outer edges with the color specified. If there are two or more pieces, follow the instructions for assembly.

Cleaning

If projects are stitched with acrylic yarn, they may be washed by hand using warm or cool

water and a mild detergent. Place on a terry-cloth towel to air dry.

Plastic Canvas Stitches

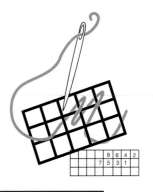

CONTINENTAL STITCH For the continental stitch, your needle comes up at 1 and all odd-numbered holes and goes down at 2 and all even-numbered holes.

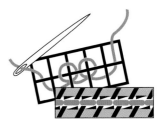

BACKSTITCH Work the plastic canvas backstitch just as you do a cross-stitch backstitch. (See page 6, Figure D.)

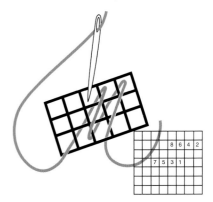

SLANTING GOBELIN STITCH For the slanting gobelin stitch, your needle comes up at 1 and all odd-numbered holes and goes down at 2 and all even-numbered holes.

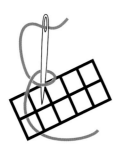

FRENCH KNOT For the French knot, bring your needle up at a hole and wrap yarn clockwise around needle. Holding the yarn, insert needle in the hole to the right and slowly pull yarn through the knot.

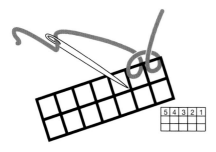

OVERCAST STITCH For the overcast stitch, the needle goes down at the numbered holes, and the yarn wraps over the edge of the canvas. Make sure to cover the canvas completely.

Ribbon Embroidery

Ribbon embroidery is much like regular embroidery or crewel work, except you use silk or silklike ribbon instead of yarn or floss. Be careful to keep ribbon untwisted as you work. You will work much looser stitches than in traditional embroidery.

Cut ribbon to 12- to 14-inch lengths, angle-cutting the ends

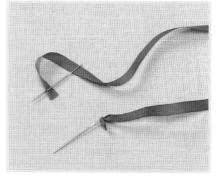

of the ribbon. Thread the ribbon through the eye of the needle, and about ½ inch from the end, pierce through the center of the ribbon with the needle. Pull the other end of ribbon until the ribbon "locks" into place.

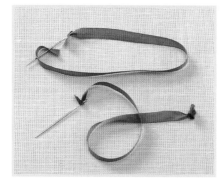

To knot the end of the ribbon, double the very end of the ribbon and pierce the end with the point of the needle. Pull the ribbon through, forming a knot.

To finish stitching, either tie off ribbon next to the fabric or make a few small backstitches and trim the tail. If you plan on washing your finished project, use a drop of washable glue to keep cut ends of ribbon from fraying.

Ribbon Embroidery Stitches

LAZY DAISY Bring needle and thread up through back of fabric, and hold ribbon with your finger on top of fabric. Being sure not to

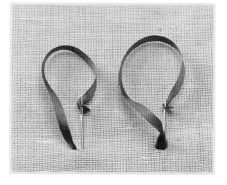

twist ribbon, reinsert needle next to the entry hole to make a loop. Bring needle up at inside of loop, go over top of loop, and insert needle at outside end of loop.

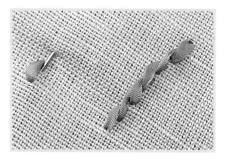

STEM STITCH Keeping ribbon untwisted, work from left to right making even, small stitches. Come up in the middle of the first stitch and down half the length past the end of the first stitch. Continue stitching for length indicated.

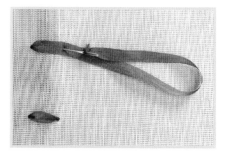

JAPANESE RIBBON STITCH Bring needle and ribbon up from behind cloth, and lay ribbon on fabric. Keeping ribbon flat, insert needle at end of stitch. Pull needle through to back of fabric.

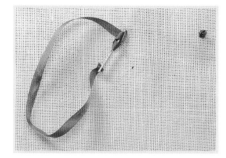

FRENCH KNOT Bring needle and ribbon up through back of fabric. Wrap ribbon around needle twice, and reinsert needle next to starting point. Slowly pull needle through ribbon.

LOOP FLOWER Form loops by bringing needle and ribbon up through back of fabric and reinserting needle next to starting point. Keep ribbon untwisted, and leave enough ribbon loop to create a petal. While making next loop, hold first loop so you don't pull it through. Continue making five loops to create flower.

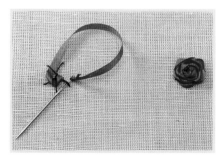

SPIDERWEB ROSE Use embroidery floss to make a five-spoked star. Thread needle with ribbon, and bring needle and ribbon up from back of fabric at middle of star. Weave ribbon over and under star points to create rose.

Woodworking

A band saw and a scroll saw are very handy, easy-to-use tools for the home workshop. They may be easily operated by a man, woman, or even an older teen with adult supervision.

Respect your saw—Safety First! Before you begin, read your instruction manual. And always keep in mind these simple safety hints when using any saw:

- Keep your work area clean and uncluttered.
- Don't use saw in damp or wet locations.
- Keep your work area well lit.
- Do not force saw through items that it is not designed for.
- Wear proper clothing— nothing loose or baggy.
- Wear safety goggles.
- Never leave a saw unattended.

Decorative Painting

Decorative painting has been handed down from generation to generation. It's an art form that was developed by untrained artists, and no artistic talent or drawing skills are necessary. Once you start painting arts and craft projects, you'll be hooked. You will surprise yourself with what you can create.

There is a large variety of styles and finishes to choose from in the following pages. Many can be completed in only a few hours. These pages will walk you through some common techniques.

Supplies

PAINTS Acrylic paints are available at your local arts and crafts stores in a wide variety of colors and brands. Mix and match your favorite colors to paint the projects in this book. These projects will work with any acrylic paint brands. Acrylic paint dries in minutes, allowing projects to be completed in no time at all. Clean hands and brushes with soap and water.

Some projects may require a medium that is not acrylic or water based. These require mineral spirits to clean up. Always check the manufacturer's label before working with a product so you can have the proper supplies available.

FINISHES Choose from a wide variety of types and brands of varnishes to protect your finished project. Varnish is available in both spray and brush-on.

Brush-on water-base varnishes dry in minutes and clean up with soap and water. Use over any acrylic paints. Don't use over paints or mediums requiring mineral spirits clean up.

Spray varnishes can be used over any type of paint or medium. For projects with a pure white surface, choose a nonyellowing varnish, though the slight yellowing of some varnishes can actually enhance certain projects for a richer look. Varnishes are available in matte, satin, or gloss finishes. Choose the shine you prefer.

BRUSHES Foam (sponge) brushes work well to seal, basecoat, and varnish wood. Clean foam brushes with soap and water when using acrylic paints and mediums. For paints or mediums that require mineral spirits to clean up, you will have to throw the disposable brush away.

Synthetic brushes work well with acrylic paints for details and designs. Use a liner brush for thin lines and details. A script brush is needed for extra long lines. Round brushes fill in round areas, do stroke work, and make broad lines. An angle brush is used to fill in large areas and to float, or side-load, color. A large flat brush is used to apply basecoat and varnish. Small flat brushes are for stroke work and basecoating small areas.

Specialty brushes, including a stencil brush and a fabric round scrubber, can be used for stencil painting and stippling. The Kemper tool or an old toothbrush can be used to spatter paint.

Wood Preparation

Properly preparing the wood piece can make all the difference in the outcome. Having a smooth surface to work on will allow you to complete the project quickly and easily. Once the wood is prepared, you are ready to proceed with a basecoat, stain, or finish, according to the project instructions. Some finishes, such as crackling, will not need the

wood sealed before applying. Always read instructions completely before starting.

Supplies you will need to prepare the wood: sandpaper (#200) for removing roughness; tack cloth, which is a sticky resin-treated cheesecloth, to remove dust after sanding; a wood sealer to seal wood and prevent warping; and a foam or 1-inch flat brush to apply sealer.

Note: Wood with knot holes requires a special sealer to prevent sap from later bleeding through the paint. Check the manufacturer's label for proper usage.

1 Choose a clear wood sealer for transparent finishes. Any rough edges should be presanded using #200 sandpaper. Wipe wood clean with a tack cloth. Use a foam or large flat brush to apply sealer. Allow sealer to dry completely. You can use a hair dryer to speed drying time, if desired.

2 Once the wood has been sealed and is dry, the grain will raise slightly. Sand with #200 sandpaper to smooth surface. Rub your hand across the surface to check for any missed rough spots. Wipe surface with a tack cloth to remove dust particles.

Transferring Designs

You don't have to know anything about drawing to transfer a design. The designs in this book can be transferred directly onto the project surface.

TRANSFER SUPPLIES Transparent tracing paper, pencil or fine marker, scissors, tape, transfer

paper (carbon or graphite), and stylus.

1 Place transparent tracing paper over the design you want to copy. Trace the design lines with a pencil or fine marker. Trace only the lines you absolutely need to complete the project. The transparent paper allows you to easily position the pattern on the wood project. Cut paper to the shape or size that is easiest to work with. Tape a few edges down on the wood surface to hold the pattern in place.

2 Place a piece of transfer paper, carbon side down, between the wood and pattern. Choose a color that will show on your project. Use a stylus or pencil to trace over the design lines. Lift a corner of the pattern to make sure the design is transferring properly.

Basic Painting Techniques
THIN LINES

1 Thin paint with 50 percent water for a fluid consistency that flows off the brush. It should be about the consistency of ink.

2 Use a liner brush for short lines and tiny details or a script brush for long lines. Dip brush into thinned paint. Wipe excess on palette.

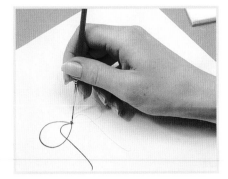

3 Hold brush upright, with handle pointing to the ceiling. Use your little finger as a balance when painting. Don't apply pressure for extra thin lines.

FLOATING COLOR This technique is also called side loading. It is used to shade or highlight the edge of an object. Floated color is a gradual blend of color to water.

1 Moisten an angle brush with water. Blot excess water from brush, setting bristles on paper towel until shine of water disappears.

2 Dip the long corner of angle brush into paint. Load paint sparingly. Carefully stroke brush on palette until color blends halfway across the brush. If the paint blends all the way to short side, clean and load again. For a thicker paint line, dilute first with 50 percent water.

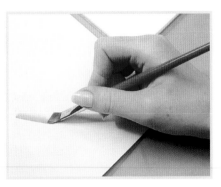

3 Hold the brush at a 45-degree angle, and using a light touch, apply color to designated area.

SPATTERING Little dots of paint are sprinkled on the surface, which is great for creating snow, aged fly spec look, or just adding fun colors to a finish. Always test spattering on paper first.

1 Thin paint with 50 to 80 percent water. Use an old toothbrush and palette knife or a Kemper tool. Dip brush into thinned paint. Lots of paint on the brush will create large dots. As the paint runs out, the dots become finer.

2 With a toothbrush, drag your thumb or palette knife across the top of the bristles, causing them to bend. As you release them, the bristles spring forward, spattering paint onto the surface.

ALTERNATIVES A Kemper tool is a tiny wire brush with a heavier wire that bends the bristles as you twist the handle. Hold the brush over the object, and twist the handle.

Hold a large flat brush vertically in one hand over the surface. Hold the handle of another brush under it horizontally. Tap handle against handle.

DOTS Perfect round dots can be made with any round implement. The size of the implement determines the size of the dot. You can use the wooden end of a brush, a stylus tip, a pencil tip, or the eraser end of pencil (with an unused eraser).

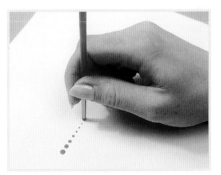

1 Use undiluted paint for thick dots or dilute paint with 50 percent water for smooth dots. Dip the tip into paint and then onto the surface. For uniform dots, you must redip in paint for each dot. For graduated dots, continue dotting with same paint load. Clean tip on paper towel after each group, and reload.

Bows and Ribbons

There are many ways to make bows, and the more you make, the easier it becomes. Cutting the ribbon ends at an angle lends a more polished appearance to the finished product.

Making a Multiloop Bow

1 Unroll several yards from a bolt of ribbon. Form loops of the ribbon with your dominant hand. Pinch the center of the loops with the thumb and forefinger of your other hand as you work.

2 Continue to add loops to your bow. Keep pinching the bow's center with your thumb and forefinger. After you have all the loops you want, trim away the excess ribbon from the bolt. If you want streamers, leave the ribbon ends long.

3 Insert a length of wire around the center of the bow. Twist the two wire ends tightly around the bow's center to eliminate loop slippage. Attach the bow to the project with the wire. You can also trim the wire and glue the bow in place.

Note: When using heavier ribbon, use a chenille stem to secure the bow. The tiny hairs on the stem will hold the bow securely and not allow twisting. For tiny, delicate bows, use thin cloth-covered wire for securing. It eliminates slipping, and it disappears into the bow loops.

Wearables

Prewash fabrics, but don't use fabric softeners, which prevent adhesives and paint from bonding with the fibers. Press out wrinkles. After you're done with your project, hand or machine wash in lukewarm water—NOT COLD—on delicate/knit cycle. Tumble dry on low for a few minutes to remove wrinkles, then remove and lay flat to dry. Do not use delicate care wash products; regular detergent is fine to use.

Sewing

The excitement of making your own crafts sometimes gets in the way of your preparation. Before plunging into your chosen project, check to make sure you have all the materials needed. Being prepared will make your sewing easier and more fun. Most of the items you need will probably be on hand already.

FABRIC The type of fabric best suited to the project is given in the list of materials. But don't hesitate to make substitutions, taking into consideration your preferences in colors and patterns. Keep in mind the scale of a pattern relative to the size of the project. The weight of the fabric is also an important consideration: Don't substitute a heavy, stiff fabric for a delicate fabric.

Invest in the best materials you can afford. Many inexpensive fabrics are less likely to be colorfast. Avoid the regret that goes with choosing a fabric that isn't quite perfect but is less expensive than the fabric you really love.

FUSIBLE ADHESIVE (OR WEBBING) A lightweight fusible iron-on adhesive is time-saving and easy to use. The adhesive is placed paper side up on the wrong side of the material. Place iron on paper, and press for one to three seconds. Allow fabric to cool. A design can then be drawn or traced onto the paper side, and cut out. Remove the paper, place the material right side up in the desired position on the project, and iron for three to five seconds.

IRONING BOARD AND STEAM IRON
Sometimes you do more sewing with the iron than you do with the sewing machine. Keeping your fabrics, seams, and hems pressed cuts down on stitches and valuable time. A steam or dry iron is best. Be sure your ironing board is well padded and has a clean covering. The iron is also used to adhere the fusible adhesive. Keep the bottom of the iron clean and free of any substance that could mark the fabric. The steam iron may be used directly on most fabrics with no shine. Test a small piece of the fabric first. If it causes a shine, iron on the reverse side.

SCISSORS Two styles are needed. One is about eight to ten inches long with a bent handle for cutting fabric. This style of scissors allows you to cut through the fabric while the fabric lays flat. These shears should be sharp and used only for fabric. The second style of scissors is smaller, about six inches, with sharp points. You will need these for smaller projects and close areas.

SEWING MACHINE Neat, even stitches are achieved in a very few minutes with a sewing machine; it helps you complete your project with ease. If desired, you can machine-stitch a zigzag stitch around the attached fusible adhesive pieces to secure the edges.

STRAIGHT PINS Nonrusting dressmaker pins are best. They will not leave rust marks on your fabric if they come in contact with dampness or glue. And dressmaker's pins have very sharp points for easy insertion.

TAPE MEASURE This should be plastic coated so that it will not stretch and can be wiped off if it comes in contact with paint or glue.

THREAD Have mercerized sewing thread in the colors needed for each project you have chosen. Proper shade and strength (about 50 weight) of thread avoids having the stitching show more than is necessary and will give the item a more finished look.

WORK SURFACE Your sewing surface should be a comfortable height for sitting and roomy enough to lay out your projects. Keep it clean and free of other crafting materials that could accidently spill or soil your fabric.

Quilting

Material Selection

BATTING Many types of batting are available to meet the needs of different projects. In general, use polyester batting with a low or medium loft. Polyester is best if the quilt will be washed frequently. All-cotton batting is preferred by some quilters for a very flat, traditional quilt. For a puffier quilt, you can use a high-loft batting, but it is difficult to quilt.

FABRIC Select only 100 percent cotton fabrics for the face and back of the quilt. Cotton is easy to cut, mark, sew, and press. Fabrics that contain synthetics are more difficult to handle and are more likely to pucker.

The backing fabric should be similar in fiber content and care instructions to the fabrics used in the quilt top. Some wide cottons (90 and 108 inches) are sold specifically for quilt backings, eliminating the need to piece the back.

THREAD Old, weak thread tangles and knots, making it frustrating to work with. Buy 100 percent cotton thread or good, long-staple polyester thread for piecing, appliqué, and machine quilting. Cotton quilting thread is wonderful for hand quilting, but it should not be used for machine quilting because it is stiff and will tend to lie on the surface of the quilt.

For piecing by hand or by machine, select a neutral thread color that blends in with most of the fabrics in the quilt. For most projects, either khaki or gray thread works well. Use white thread for basting, do not risk using colored thread, which could leave color behind. For appliqué, the thread should match the fabric that is being appliquéd to the background. The color of quilting thread is a personal design choice. If you want your quilting to show up, use a contrasting thread color.

Tools

NEEDLES The needles used for hand piecing and hand appliqué are called sharps. For hand quilting, use betweens (generally, start with a size 8 and work toward using a size 10 or 12). Use the smallest needle you can to make the smallest stitches.

Always use a sharp needle on your sewing machine; a dull

needle will skip stitches and snag the threads of the fabric, creating puckers.

PINS Use fine, sharp straight pins (such as silk pins) for piecing and holding appliqué pieces in place before basting or stitching. Long quilter's pins are used to hold the three layers (top, batting, and backing) before they are basted together or quilted.

ROTARY CUTTER To cut fabric quickly and easily, invest in a rotary cutter, see-through ruler, and self-healing mat. These tools let you cut strips of fabric efficiently.

SCISSORS A sharp pair of scissors is essential for cutting fabric. Keep another, separate pair for cutting templates and other nonfabric items.

THIMBLE A quilting thimble on the third finger of your quilting hand will protect you from needle sores.

Material Preparation

WASHING Always wash fabrics first. This will remove some of the chemicals added by the manufacturer, making it easier to quilt. Also, cotton fabric does shrink, and most of the shrinkage will occur during the first washing and drying. Be sure to use settings that are as hot as those you intend to use with the finished quilt.

Dark, intense colors, especially reds, tend to bleed or run. Wash these fabrics by themselves. If the water becomes colored, try soaking the fabric in a solution of three parts cold water to one part

white wine vinegar. Rinse thoroughly. Wash again. If the fabric is still losing its color, discard the fabric and select another. It is not worth using a fabric that may ruin the other fabrics when the finished quilt is washed.

MARKING AND CUTTING FABRIC

To cut fabric the traditional way for piecing or appliqué, place the pattern right side down on the wrong side of the fabric. Trace around the pattern with a hard-lead pencil or a colored pencil designed for marking on fabric. Cut around each piece with sharp fabric scissors.

In many cases, it is faster and easier to cut fabric using a rotary cutter. This tool, which looks and works like a pizza cutter, must be used with a self-healing mat and a see-through ruler. Always use the safety shield of the cutter when it is not in use.

Fold the fabric in half lengthwise with selvages together. Adjust fabric until it hangs straight. The line that is created by the fold is parallel to the fabric's straight of grain. Keeping this fold in place, lay the fabric on the mat. Place a see-through ruler on the fabric. Align one of the ruler's grid lines with the fold, and trim the uneven edge of the fabric. Apply steady, even pressure to the rotary cutter and to the ruler to keep them and the fabric from shifting. Do not let the cutter get farther away from you than the hand that is holding the ruler.

To cut pieces, reposition the ruler so that it covers the width of the strip to be cut, with the

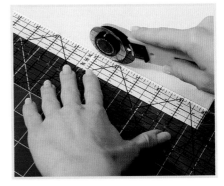

trimmed edge on the markings for the appropriate measurement on the ruler.

After cutting the strip, hold it up to make sure it is straight. If it is angled, refold the fabric and trim it again. Continue cutting strips, checking frequently that the strips are straight.

Piecing the Quilt

Unless otherwise noted, all seam allowances for projects in this book are ¼ inch. All projects in this book call for machine piecing. Hand piecing will work just as well, but it will take more time. When piecing, accuracy is important. A small error repeated in each block, or worse, in each seam, will become a large distortion. Before starting a large project, make a sample block and measure it. Is it the desired size? If not, figure out where the inaccuracy occurred. Are any seams a few threads too wide or narrow? Clip seams, and restitch.

When machine piecing, set the sewing machine's stitch length to 10 to 13 stitches per inch (or between 2 and 3 on machines that do not use the stitches-per-inch measure). Stitch across each seam allowance, along the seam line, and across the seam

allowance at the far end of the seam. Do not backstitch. Make sure the seam allowance is consistently ¼ inch.

Preparation for Quilting

Once you have made the blocks, sewn them together, and added borders according to the directions in the project, then it is time to quilt.

Decide what designs you will be quilting. For a traditional look, outline important elements of the design with quilting. A grid of stitching works well in background areas. Fancier design elements that complement the theme of the quilt can also be incorporated. Make sure there will be some stitching every few inches to secure the batting so that it does not shift.

Decide now if you need to mark the top for quilting. Simple outlining or grids can be marked with masking tape as you quilt. For more elaborate designs, mark the top of the quilt with the lightest mark possible. Dark marks may be difficult to remove when the quilt is finished.

Spread out the backing (right side down) on a table or other flat surface. Use masking tape to

secure it after smoothing it out. Place the batting on top of the backing, smoothing it out also. Finally, place the completed quilt top on the backing, right side up. Stretch it out so it is smooth, and tape it.

For hand quilting, baste the layers together. For best results, start basting at the center of the quilt and work toward the edges. Create a grid of basting by making a line of stitching approximately every four inches.

For machine quilting, baste by hand as described above or use safety pins. Place a safety pin every three or four inches. To save time later, avoid placing pins on quilting lines.

Quilting

Quilting (stitching that goes through all three layers of the quilt) is both functional and decorative. It holds the batting in place. It is also an important design element, enhancing the texture of the finished quilt.

To outline design areas, stitch ¼ inch away from each seam line. Simply decide where to stitch by eye or use ¼-inch masking tape placed along each seam as a guide. Masking tape can also

be used as guides for straight lines and grids. Stitch beside the edge of the tape, avoiding stitching through the tape and getting the adhesive on the needle and thread. Do not leave the masking tape on the fabric when you are finished stitching each day, however, because it can leave a sticky residue that is difficult to remove.

HAND QUILTING Some quilters hold their work unsupported in their lap when they quilt. Most quilters, however, prefer to use some sort of quilting hoop or frame to hold the quilt stretched out. This makes it easier to stitch with an even tension and helps to prevent puckering and tucks.

Use no more than 18 inches of quilting thread at once. Longer pieces of thread tend to tangle, and the end gets worn as it is pulled through the fabric. Knot the end of the thread with a quilter's knot. Slip the needle into the quilt top and batting about an inch from where the first stitch should start. Pull the needle up through the quilt top at the beginning of the first stitch. Hold the thread firmly, and give it a little tug. The knot should pop into the batting and lodge between the quilt top and backing.

The quilt stitch is a running stitch. Place your free hand (left hand for right-handed people) under the quilt to feel for the needle as it pokes through. Load the needle with a couple of stitches by rocking the needle back and forth through the fabric. At first, focus on making

evenly sized stitches. Also, make sure you are going through all three layers. When you have mastered that, work on making the stitches smaller.

MACHINE QUILTING Machine quilting is easy to learn, but it does take some practice. Make a few trial runs before starting to stitch on your completed quilt. On the test swatch, adjust the tension settings so that the stitches are even and do not pucker or have loose loops of thread.

The easiest machine stitching is long, straight lines, starting at the center of the quilt and radiating out. These lines may be a grid, stitched in the ditches formed by the seams, outlines around design elements, or channels (long, evenly spaced lines).

Whatever the pattern, quilt from the center to the outer edges. Plan the order of stitching before you begin. Your plan should minimize the need to start and stop.

Before placing the quilt on the sewing machine, roll the sides in toward the center and secure with pins or bicycle clips. Use an even-feed walking foot for straight lines of stitching. For freehand stitching,

use a darning foot and lower the feed dogs or use a throat plate that covers the feed dogs.

To begin, turn the handwheel by hand to lower and raise the needle to its highest point. Pull gently on the top thread to bring the bobbin thread up through the quilt. Stitch in place for several stitches. Gradually increase the length of each stitch for the first ½ inch of quilting, until the stitches are the desired length. This will secure the ends of the thread, making it unnecessary to backstitch or knot them. Reverse these steps at the end of each quilting line.

When quilting with the even-feed walking foot, place your hands on the quilt on either side of the presser foot and apply even pressure. Keep the layers smooth and free of tucks.

Binding the Quilt

Binding may be made from strips of fabric that match or coordinate with the fabrics used in the quilt. These strips may be cut on the straight grain or on the bias. Straight binding is easier to cut and apply and can be used on most of the projects in this book. Quilts that have curved edges require bias binding. Bias binding is stronger and tends to last longer. You can also purchase quilt binding. Apply according to the manufacturer's instructions.

To make straight binding, cut strips of fabric 3¼ inches wide on the lengthwise or crosswise grain. For each side of the quilt, you will need a strip the length of that side plus two inches.

Baste ¼ inch from the outer edge all around the quilt. Make sure all corners are square, and trim any excess batting or fabric. Prepare each strip of binding by folding it in half lengthwise, wrong sides together, and press. Find the center of each strip. Also find the center of each side of the quilt.

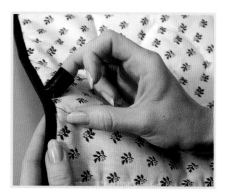

Place the binding strip on top of the quilt, aligning the raw edges of the strip and of the quilt and matching the centers. Stitch a ½-inch seam from one end of the quilt to the other. If you use an even-feed walking foot instead of the regular presser foot, it will be easier to keep the binding and the quilt smooth.

Trim the excess binding from each end. Fold the binding to the back of the quilt, and slipstitch it in place. Repeat for the opposite side of the quilt. Attach the binding to the ends of the quilt using the same procedure, except do not trim the ends of the binding. Instead, fold the excess binding over the end of the quilt. Holding the end in place, fold the binding to the back of the quilt and slip-stitch in place.

Rubber Stamping

RUBBER STAMPS Look for two general styles of images: solid and line-art. A solid image lets you quickly get a lot of color onto a surface. A line-art image may look like cartoon art or a fine pen-and-ink drawing.

INKS Begin with ink pads that use standard, dye-based ink. These are water-based inks. Dye-based inks are easy to use, and the ink dries quickly. Pigment ink is thick, opaque, and slow-drying—not good for slick surfaces, but perfect for embossing. Pigment ink also works well when stamping on colored paper because the color of the paper won't show through.

Techniques

STAMPING Tap the stamp gently two or three times on a pad. Turn it over to see how well it's inked. Stamp it on scrap paper to get a feel for applying the right amount of ink. Too little ink causes details to be lost and colors to look pale, while too much obscures details. New stamps usually require heavier inking the first time around.

Make a stamp impression by gently and evenly applying the inked stamp to the paper. Do not grind or rock the stamp.

Clean off each die before you switch from one color to another and after you're finished using it. Use a damp paper towel to clean ink off stamps. Never use alcohol-based solvents or other harsh cleansing agents. Store stamps with the stamp side down, out of direct sunlight and away from dust.

EMBOSSING Embossing creates a stunning look. Use only pigment or embossing ink, and use only an embossing gun as your heating tool. Embossing thickens the line, so don't expect sharp images.

To emboss, ink the image on a pigment ink pad and stamp it. Put a sheet of paper on your work area. Hold the stamped image over the sheet and dust the image liberally with embossing powder. Tilt the image so the excess powder falls onto the catch sheet. (Return the excess to the bottle.) Direct the hot-air flow of the embossing gun (about six inches away from the stamped sheet) back and forth across the image until the powder melts.

Country Heart Sachet

Add a touch of fragrance to your home with a country heart sachet. Elegant silk ribbon embroidery graces the felt heart.

WHAT YOU'LL NEED

6×6-inch tear-away

Pencil

9×12-inch felt pieces: ½ piece
  Wedgwood blue, ½ piece
  antique white

Water-erasable marker

Scissors

Pins

Embroidery ribbon
  (see color key)

#20 chenille needle

6-strand cotton embroidery floss:
  ecru, pink

Potpourri

8-inch length dusty rose ribbon,
  ⅜ inch wide

⁷/₁₆-inch button

Ribbon Color	YLI	Width
— Dark green	021	4mm
— Light green	060	4mm
— Gold	54	4mm
— Rose	113	4mm
— Blue	126	7mm

1 Trace pattern onto tear-away. Use marker to trace large heart twice on Wedgwood blue felt. Cut out hearts. Trim pattern along smaller heart outline. Trace and cut out small heart of antique white felt. Pin or baste tear-away pattern to white heart.

2 Work embroidery through tear-away according to photo and diagrams. Use 2 strands ecru floss to work spokes for spider web rose. Stitch flowers, then vine. Add leaves and French knots last. Remove pattern by gently tearing it away from under stitching.

3 Center and pin embroidered heart onto a blue heart. Attach white heart to blue with blanket stitch and 6 strands pink floss.

4 Blanket stitch blue hearts together with 6 strands ecru floss. Stop stitching about ¾ of way around hearts; fill with potpourri. Finish stitching hearts together.

5 Fold dusty rose ribbon in half, turning up ends about ½ inch. Position ends on back of stuffed heart at top center, with folded ends inside. Use 6 strands ecru floss to tack ribbon to heart and to sew button on front.

Pattern is 100 percent.

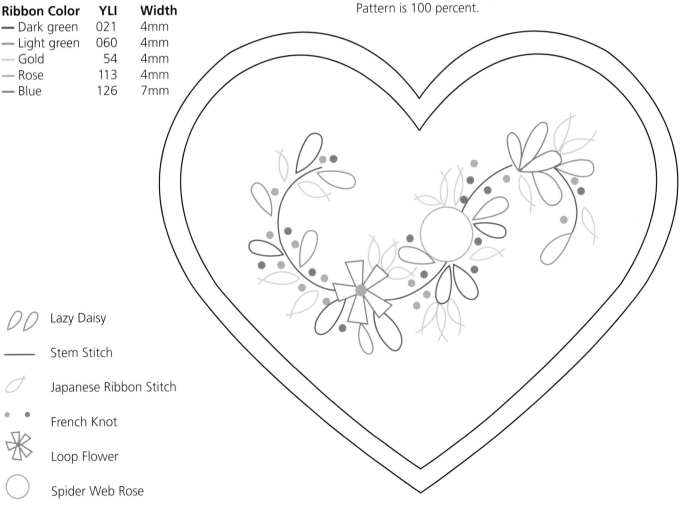

Lazy Daisy

Stem Stitch

Japanese Ribbon Stitch

French Knot

Loop Flower

Spider Web Rose

Morning Glory Birdhouse

The rustic charm of this flowered birdhouse

will captivate visitors in your backyard.

WHAT YOU'LL NEED

36×3½-inch stained fence post

4×6-inch stained birdhouse

Hot glue gun, glue sticks

6 stems preserved plumosus fern

6-foot silk blue morning
   glory vine

Staple gun, staples

6 to 8 stems honeysuckle vines

Sheet moss

Hammer, nails (optional)

3 Staple morning glory vine up fence post and around birdhouse; face flowers in different directions for a natural look.

1 Hot glue or nail birdhouse 11 inches from top of fence post.

2 Cut and hot glue fern up fence post and around birdhouse.

4 Hot glue honeysuckle vines and moss throughout arrangement.

Antique Watering Can

This elegant watering can creates a new country look

with roses, larkspur, and hydrangeas.

1 Foam should be a little taller than the lip of the watering can. Glue foam in place in can.

3 Cut dried roses 4 to 8 inches long. Insert yellow roses in center, in front of handle, staggering rose heights. Insert dark pink roses in front of and around yellow roses.

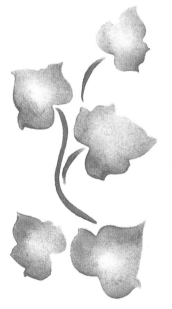

2 Cut larkspur, nigella, and oregano 10 to 15 inches long. Insert groups at center of can behind handle. Insert larkspur in center first, making it the tallest.

4 Cut hydrangea 3 to 4 inches long and insert around edges of container, securing with hot glue if necessary. Fill in any bare spots with oregano.

Sunflower Garden

Bright silk sunflowers are the focal point of this country wreath.

Let the warm, sunny tones evoke a cozy feeling in your home.

1 Cut sunflower stems to approximately 1 to 2 inches. Cut apart poppy and chrysanthemum stems, and trim individual flower stems to about 5 inches. Cut off all leaves from sunflower stems, and retain.

2 Cut bittersweet into separate stems. Insert bittersweet stems into wreath. Wrap and bend stems around wreath. Glue in place if necessary to hold.

4 Glue heads of yellow sunflowers into wreath. Put hot glue on back of flower head, and push flower into wreath. Form a triangular pattern with yellow sunflowers first, then glue 3 rust sunflowers between yellow sunflowers. Keep heads of flowers as flat on wreath as possible.

5 Glue individual leaves around sunflowers to hide glue.

3 Insert poppies into wreath between bittersweet. Space flowers evenly around wreath. Repeat this with chrysanthemums, leaving open spaces for sunflowers. Add hot glue to flower stems to secure.

Variations

This wreath can also be used as a candle ring around a glass hurricane. Any variety of country-style silk flowers can be used to complement the sunflowers. The best choices are flowers that are smaller than the sunflowers. For a brighter wreath, use only yellow sunflowers. A bow made of ribbon or raffia can also be added, if desired. A country print ribbon, such as gingham, would enhance the quaint country charm of this wreath.

Flag Fanfare

Celebrate your love for America with an Americana

classic—a flag quilt! It truly conveys the pioneer spirit.

WHAT YOU'LL NEED

⅝ yard red fabric

1⅔ yards white fabric

Self-healing mat, rotary cutter, see-through ruler

Scissors

Sewing machine

White thread

Iron, ironing board

¾ yard blue fabric

72 various white buttons

Sewing needle

½ yard black fabric

1½ yards backing fabric

42×42 inches batting

1-inch safety pins

Washable marking pencil

Quilting needle, quilting thread

½ yard binding fabric

1 For center star section: Cut 20 red 2×2-inch squares and 16 white 3½×2-inch rectangles. Draw a diagonal line corner to corner on the wrong side of 16 red squares.

2 (Unless otherwise noted, all seam allowances are ¼ inch and all pieces are matched right sides together. After sewing, press all seams to darkest fabric.) Lay a 2-inch red diagonal-marked square on the right side of a 3½×2-inch white rectangle, matching corners. Sew along diagonal, and trim fabric ½ inch from seam line. Make 16 pieces.

3 Following diagram below, sew pieces together to make a star block. Make 4 blocks. Sew 4 star blocks together to make a large center stars block.

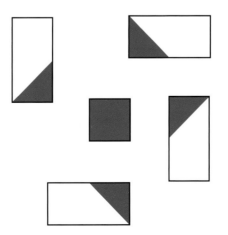

4 For flag: Cut 4 blue 9½×5-inch rectangles, 4 white 2×18½-inch strips, 8 red 2×18½-inch strips, 8 white 2×9½-inch strips, 4 red 2×9½-inch strips.

5 Sew together a white, red, and white 2×9½-inch strip. Make 4. Sew each set to the right side of a blue 9½×5-inch rectangle (piece A). Sew together a red, white, and red 2×18½-inch strip. Make 4. Sew each block to bottom of a piece A to create a flag. Sew buttons to blue section of flag. Sew flags around center stars block.

6 For accent border: Cut 4 black 1½-inch strips selvage to selvage. Measure vertically through center of flags block, and cut 2 strips this measurement. Sew strips to sides of flags block. Measure horizontally through center, and cut 2 strips this measurement. Sew strips to top and bottom of block.

7 For bear paw corners: Cut 20 white 2½-inch squares, 12 white 2⅞-inch squares (cut in half diagonally), 16 white 4½-inch squares, 4 white 4⅞-inch squares (cut in half diagonally), 4 white 9×12-inch rectangles, 4 blue 9×12-inch rectangles.

8 To make speedy triangles: Place a white and blue 9×12-inch rectangle right sides together. Draw a grid on rectangle of twelve 2⅞-inch squares. Draw a diagonal line through each corner of every square. Sew ¼ inch away from diagonal line, on both sides of line. Cut on all solid lines (see diagram below). Repeat with remaining 9×12-inch white and blue rectangles.

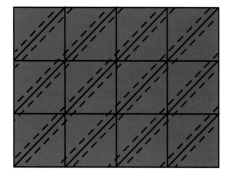

9 Assemble 12 bear paw sets according to diagram A. Assemble 8 bear paw sets according to diagram B. Assemble 4 bear paw sets according to diagram C.

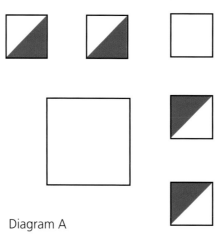

Diagram A

Diagram B

Diagram C

10 Assemble 4 corners according to finished photo. When joining, right sides are even. Add corners to center flags block. Put opposite corners on first (top and bottom) and then the remaining 2 corners.

11 Cut backing and batting 2 inches larger than quilt face. Place backing fabric face-down on surface; place batting on top. Place quilt top faceup on batting. Pin baste with 1-inch safety pins. Mark quilting design with washable marking pencil. Starting in center, quilt with small even stitches. Trim batting and backing even with quilt face.

12 For binding: Cut six 2½-inch-wide strips the width of fabric. Join all strips end to end. Fold in half lengthwise, wrong sides together, and press. Measuring through center of quilt lengthwise, cut 2 strips this length plus 2 inches. On 1 long side of each measured and cut strip, fold in ½ inch and press. The ½-inch folded in will give your binding a clean, finished edge. On front of quilt, with raw edges even, stitch a strip to each side. After stitching, fold the binding over the seam allowance to the back. Hand-stitch to back along the seam line. Next measure through the center (widthwise), and add 1 inch to this measurement. Cut 2 strips this length. With wrong sides together press strips in half and follow same procedure as for side binding strips.

Watermelon Tote

That sweet symbol of summer—the watermelon!

Don't be surprised if someone wants your "recipe"

to make this scrumptious bag.

WHAT YOU'LL NEED

Tracing paper
Pencil
½ yard red cotton fabric
¼ yard fusible fleece
⅓ yard green cotton fabric
Scissors
Iron, ironing board
Pins
Sewing machine
Thread to match red
   and green fabrics
Sewing needle
12-inch red zipper
2 green buttons, ¾ inch each
Black thread
14 seed-shaped black buttons

1 Trace patterns on page 31. From red fabric, trace and cut out 4 melon sides; from fusible fleece, trace and cut out 2 melon sides and 1 rind; from green fabric, trace and cut out 2 rinds. Fuse a fleece side to wrong side of a red melon side; repeat. Pin a melon side without fleece to one with fleece, right sides together, and sew around shape, leaving an opening to turn. Trim fleece from seam allowance, clip curves, and turn right side out. Press. Repeat for other melon side. Hand-sew openings closed.

2 Machine-sew a heavy zigzag (bartack) over zipper teeth ¾ inch in from closed end to shorten zipper. Sew zipper to straight edges of each melon side, beginning and ending ¼ inch from edges of melon sides and allowing zipper teeth to show. Hand-sew melon sides together along top straight edge beyond zipper opening.

3 Fuse rind fleece to a green rind. Pin other rind to piece, right sides together, and sew, leaving an opening to turn. Trim fleece from seam allowance, clip curves, and turn right side out. Press. Hand-sew opening closed.

4 Matching dots on sides to ones on rind, pin melon sides to rind ¼ inch in from rind edges. Tuck zipper ends out of way of seam. With red thread in needle and green thread in bobbin, sew melon sides to rind.

5 Cut 3×36-inch piece of green fabric. Fold in half the long way, right sides together. With ¼-inch seam allowance, sew along tube (leave end open for turning). Turn right side out; press. Sew open end closed. Sew to rind at each end; sew a green button over strap at each end.

6 Using black thread, randomly sew black buttons on melon sides for seeds.

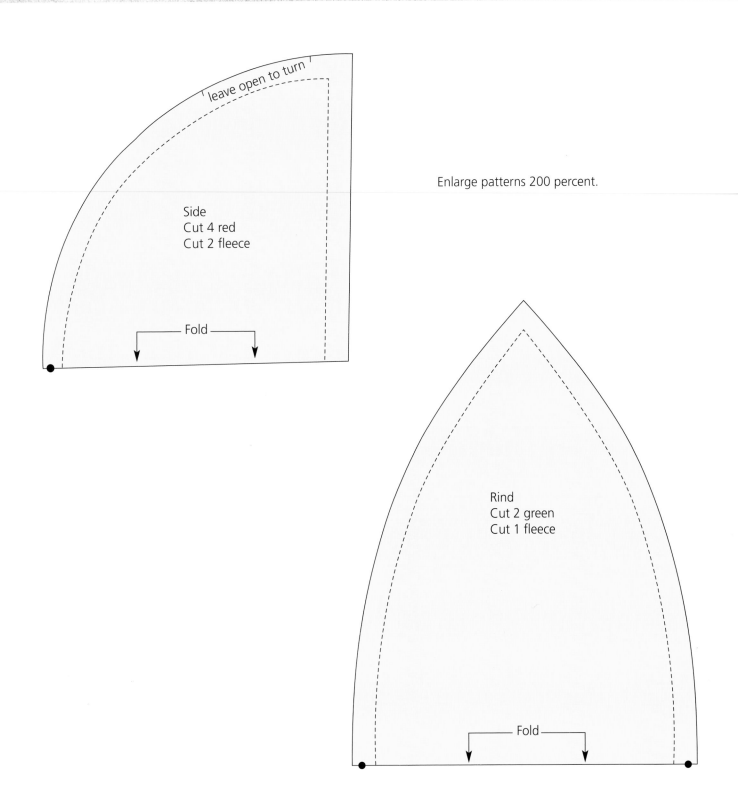

leave open to turn

Side
Cut 4 red
Cut 2 fleece

Fold

Enlarge patterns 200 percent.

Rind
Cut 2 green
Cut 1 fleece

Fold

Herb Rack

Add a fresh garden fragrance to your home and have your culinary herbs near at hand with this eye-catching aromatic herb and decorative flower rack.

WHAT YOU'LL NEED

Large wood herb rack, with
   5 hole openings
3 ounces dried lavender
3 ounces dried oregano
3 ounces preserved mountain
   mint
3 ounces dried white larkspur
20 stems dried peach roses
Heavy-duty scissors
10 strands raffia

1 Cut bundles of dried herbs and flowers 15 to 22 inches long.

3 Tie tops of each bundle with strands of raffia.

Tip

Dry your favorite summer garden herbs—such as dill, rosemary, oregano, mint, parsley, basil, and sage—for display and cooking.

2 Insert bundles through hole openings of rack. Remove any additional leaves on the bottom of the stems for easier insertion into openings.

Peach Terra-Cotta Garden

The beauty of a sun-soaked garden is captured

in this terra-cotta arrangement.

WHAT YOU'LL NEED

3×4×8-inch block dry floral foam

Hot glue gun, glue sticks

5×5×10-inch oval terra-cotta container

10 to 12 stems dried green and blue hydrangea

Wire cutters

18 to 20 dried peach roses

12 stems fresh or dried peach and mauve statice

5 to 6 stems dried pink celosia

3 ounces dried white larkspur

2½-inch floral wood picks

Green floral tape

6 stems fresh or dried lemon leaf (salal)

1 ounce dried festuca grass

1 Hot glue foam into center of container.

3 Cut dried roses, statice, celosia, and larkspur 7 to 10 inches. Make bundles, combining stems of different plants. Attach wood picks to stems of bundles, and wrap with floral tape. Insert bundles throughout container.

2 Cut stems of hydrangea 8 to 10 inches long, and insert them into foam at center and around edges of container.

4 Hot glue lemon leaf and festuca grass into open areas around arrangement.

Wonderful Jumper

Looking for a dress that's a bit fancier than your usual week-

end attire? This stylish jumper is dressy, yet so comfortable.

WHAT YOU'LL NEED

- 4 coordinating fabrics for flowers, ⅛ yard each
- Pencil
- Scissors
- Scraps of 1 or 2 green fabrics for leaves
- Needle
- Thread to match
- Denim jumper
- 4 battenburg doilies, 4 inches in diameter each
- Washable fabric glue
- Pins
- 9 small buttons to coordinate with flower fabrics
- 1 cathedral-shaped doily (optional)
- Sewing machine (optional)

1 Trace a total of 9 circles for flower yo-yos onto coordinating fabrics, and cut out. Trace and cut 10 circles from leaf fabrics.

2 With needle and thread, use a running stitch to stitch ⅛ inch from edge of each flower fabric circle. Sew on wrong side of fabric. When completely around circle, pull thread to gather edges together. Tie thread to secure. Flatten to form a fabric yo-yo. Repeat for all flowers.

3 Fold each leaf circle in half with wrong sides together. Fold the corners into the center, and finger press in place.

4 With needle and thread, use a running stitch and stitch ⅛ inch from cut edge of leaf. Pull thread tight, and secure with a knot. Repeat for all leaves.

5 Lay jumper flat. Using photo as guide for placement, place battenburg doilies in position. With washable fabric glue, secure doilies in place. Glue along all solid edges of doilies to secure bond. (If cathedral doily is to be used as a pocket on lower right of jumper, sew in place with machine.)

6 Lay out yo-yo flowers and leaves. Pin and sew in place using needle and thread. Blind-stitch around outside edge of each flower, tucking leaves underneath flowers.

7 Sew a button in center of each flower.

Tip

If you do not have the desired colors in your scraps of fabric or you just want to take a shortcut, premade cloth yo-yos are available at most craft and fabric stores.

Pattern is 100 percent.

Rose Hydrangea Wreath

Pastel colors and symbols of love and romance all come together in this beautiful arrangement. Add a touch of elegance to your house with this special wreath.

WHAT YOU'LL NEED

Evergreen wreath

Brown chenille stem

Hot glue gun, glue sticks

Ivy bush or swag at least
  36 inches long

Heavy-duty craft scissors

5 large silk red roses

3 silk rosebuds

6 silk hydrangea clusters, pink
  and white

5 silk magnolia leaves,
  4 to 5 inches each

2 yards pink paper ribbon

Floral wire, 24 gauge

Wire cutters

1 Fluff wreath by arranging branches. Twist chenille stem on back of wreath to form a hook for hanging. Glue to secure.

2 Cut ivy into sections, and place around wreath, covering about 80 percent of front of wreath. Weave ivy in and out of branches. Spot glue in place.

3 Glue 2 open roses at left side of wreath at about the 7 and 8 o'clock positions. Glue 3 open roses to right side, spacing them at the 2, 3, and 4 o'clock positions. Leave bottom middle of wreath open for bow.

4 Glue 2 rosebuds above large roses on left going up wreath. Glue a rosebud between and to right of large roses on right.

5 Glue a hydrangea cluster at bottom center of wreath (above where bow will be placed). Glue 2 hydrangea clusters between large roses on left. Glue a hydrangea cluster between bottom 2 large roses on right. Cut 1 remaining hydrangea cluster into pieces, and glue pieces randomly around wreath. (Save 1 cluster for step 7.)

6 Glue 5 magnolia leaves to bottom of wreath so they fan around hydrangea blossom. Be sure fan is large enough so that when bow is placed, it does not completely cover leaves.

7 Make a 6-loop bow with paper ribbon, and secure center with floral wire. Wire bow to wreath under bottom center hydrangea blossom. Cut bow ends into Vs. Glue last hydrangea cluster to center of bow.

Country Barn Tissue Cover

Camouflage a tissue box with a replica of a country barn!

The open barn doors reveal a contented, hay-munching cow.

This is a fun, easy plastic canvas project.

WHAT YOU'LL NEED

12×18-inch ultrastiff plastic canvas

Scissors

#18 tapestry needle

Plastic canvas yarn (see color key)

6-strand embroidery floss: gray, black

Raffia

Monofilament thread

Colors

■ Black
■ Gray
■ Red
▨ Eggshell
☐ Natural
■ Denim
▨ Pink

1 Carefully cut pieces from plastic canvas according to charts. For barn back, use pattern for front but without cutouts. Use 1 strand yarn to work all continental, slanting gobelin, overcast, and long stitches. Use 6 strands of floss to work French knots on cow: gray for nostrils and black for eyes. For barn back, work as front but without cutouts for windows and doors.

2 Use eggshell to join door and window inserts to front openings. With eggshell, join doors and windows through empty holes in inserts. Stitch randomly with raffia to fill empty holes in window insert. Work loops across bottom row. Cut loops, and trim unevenly. Insert small piece of raffia through cow's mouth where indicated on chart by green lines.

3 Use eggshell to join barn sides at corners. Use red to overcast bottom and top edges of barn.

4 Use denim to join roof pieces and to overcast opening and edges. Use monofilament thread to tack on roof where indicated on chart by Xs.

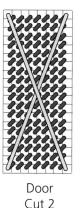

Door
Cut 2

Window
Cut 2

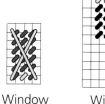

Window insert

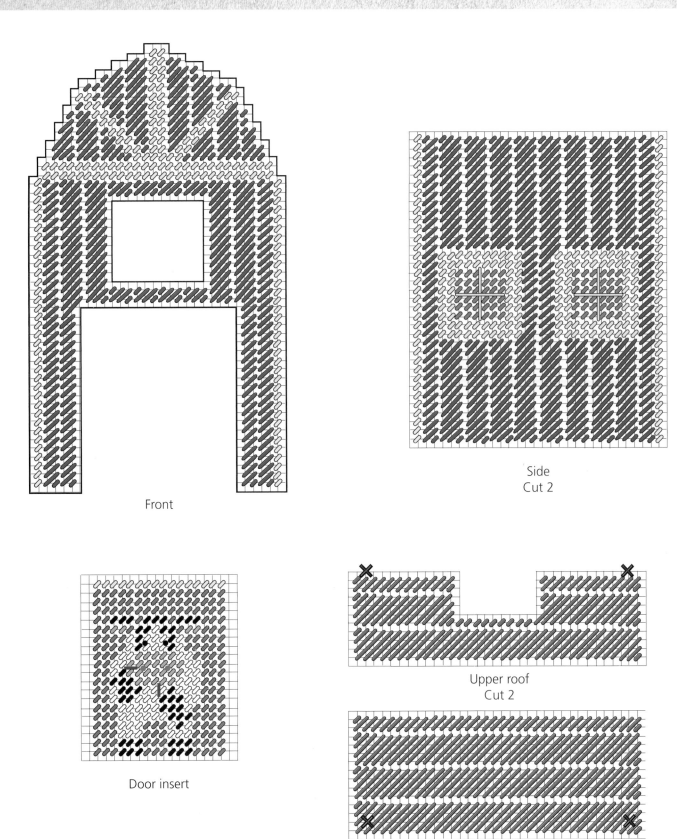

Front

Side
Cut 2

Door insert

Upper roof
Cut 2

Lower roof
Cut 2

Halloween Sweatshirt

Just because you don't want to dress up as a ghoul doesn't mean you don't want to celebrate Halloween! Sew homespun patches on this ordinary sweatshirt to make it festive.

WHAT YOU'LL NEED

½ yard light fusible webbing

⅓ yard black/rust mini-check fabric

⅓ yard rust/black plaid fabric

⅓ yard tan/beige mini-check fabric

See-through ruler

Scissors

Iron, ironing board

Embroidery floss: rust, black

Embroidery needle

Scraps: mustard calico (moon), black calico (bat, pumpkin face, cat), green calico (leaf), brown calico (stem), orange calico (pumpkin)

Tracing paper

Pencil

Black sweatshirt

Thread to match calico, checked, and plaid fabrics

Fabric glue

20 buttons, various shapes and sizes

1 Iron 6½×5-inch rectangles of fusible webbing to the black/rust mini-check, rust/black plaid, and tan/beige fabrics. Remove paper. Tear a 4×5½-inch rectangle from each fused piece.

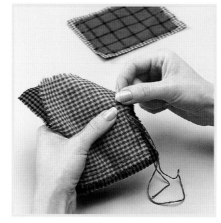

2 Tear a 3½×5-inch square from unfused portions of each fabric (that have not been fused with webbing) listed in step 1. Place small tan/beige square on top of large black/rust mini-check rectangle, place small black/rust mini-check rectangle on top of large rust/black plaid rectangle, and place small rust/black plaid on top of large tan/beige rectangle. Using 6 strands of rust floss, stitch a long running stitch around each small rectangle to secure it to bottom piece.

3 Fuse scraps of webbing to backs of scrap pieces of fabric for shapes. Trace patterns on page 45 onto paper backing, and cut out. Remove paper.

4 Position moon and bat on first square; pumpkin face, leaf, and stem on second square; and cat on third square. Fuse in place. Position squares on center front of sweatshirt, and fuse.

5 Using an appliqué stitch and matching thread, stitch around each design. Use black floss to stitch whiskers on cat by hand.

6 With scraps leftover from the plaids or mini-check fabrics, cut 2 squares 2½×2½ inches and 2 squares out of another fabric 2×2 inches. Place the smaller square on top of the larger, and stitch around the edges using

6 strands of rust floss and a long running stitch. Place a square on each sleeve, and use a straight stitch on sewing machine to sew around edges.

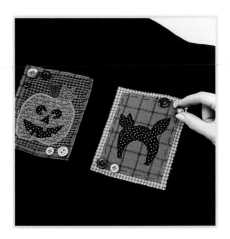

7 On front squares, glue 3 buttons to top of each square and 2 buttons in opposite corners. For squares on sleeves, glue 3 buttons in middle of 1 square and 2 buttons in other. Let glue dry overnight.

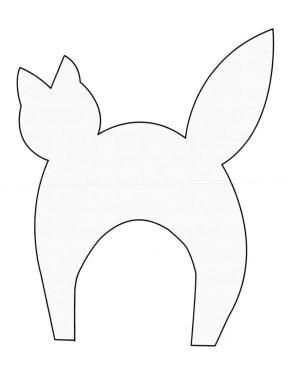

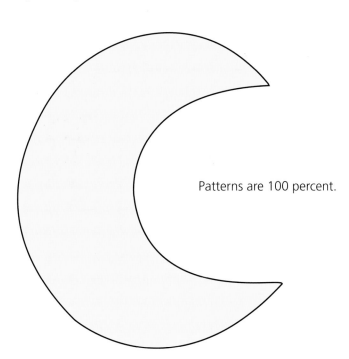

Patterns are 100 percent.

Cross-Stitch Pillow

This whimsical pillow hosts a cast of colorful country characters. What a lovely, homey touch to add to your home.

WHAT YOU'LL NEED

Premade pillow

Embroidery floss
(see color key)

Embroidery needle

Scissors

Pillow form

Small button

All cross-stitch is done with 4 strands floss and all backstitch is done with 3 strands. Backstitch bunny with black, birdhouse and flower with light brown, and bird with dark blue. Sew button on top right heart.

Color	DMC
Brick	3722
Light green	368
Dark green	367
Yellow	3822
Orange	977
Light blue	931
Dark blue	930
Black	310
White	White
Light rose	224
Dark rose	3721
Light brown	436
Dark brown	434
Ecru	822

Honey-Orange Tea Sampler

This cross-stitch sampler is a great addition to any kitchen.

It would make a lovely housewarming gift for a dear friend!

Each stitch will be made over 2 threads of linen. Stitch with 2 strands of floss and backstitch with 1 strand. Pattern overlays at side arrows. Top and bottom arrows show middle of pattern.

Color	DMC
Black	310
Green	367
Yellow	725
Cream	Ecru
Light tan	676
Dark tan	435
Brown	433
Light orange	722
Dark orange	946

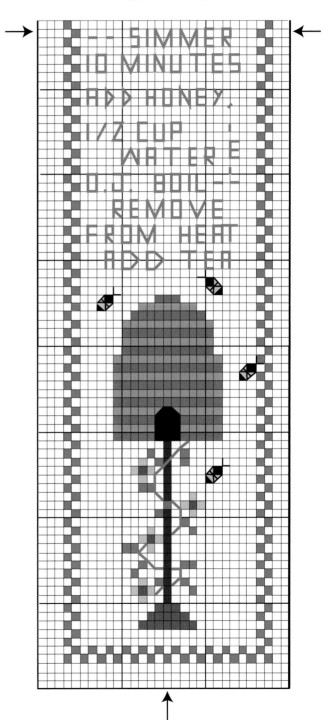

Welcome Friends Hanging Hoop

Stitch a heartfelt welcome to greet all who enter your home or kitchen.

WHAT YOU'LL NEED

Tracing paper

Pencil

Scissors

Water-erasable marker

9×12-inch felt pieces: denim blue, antique white, ½ piece cranberry, ½ piece peach

#20 chenille needle

6-strand cotton embroidery floss: blue, ecru, red

Pins

11 white sew-through buttons, ⅜ inch each

6-inch wood embroidery hoop

Craft glue

Raffia

2 small magnets

1 Trace entire pattern on page 52 onto tracing paper to make guide for placing pieces. Also trace each pattern piece separately, and cut out to make templates (or make 6 photocopies of pattern). Mark lettering with dots on scalloped circle template. Use marker to trace around templates onto felt. From denim felt cut out 2 small hearts, 1 scalloped circle; from antique white felt cut out 1 scalloped circle, 1 large outer heart; from cranberry felt cut out 1 outer teapot, 1 large inner heart; from peach felt cut out 1 inner teapot.

2 Use needle to poke holes through template at dots. Transfer lettering placement to antique white scalloped circle by marking dots through holes in template with erasable marker. Use 6 strands of blue floss to work lettering by backstitching.

3 Pin antique white and cranberry hearts on peach teapot according to finished photo. Use blue floss to blanket stitch hearts in place. Cross-stitch a button to center of heart. Pin denim blue hearts in place with blue floss. Use ecru floss to blanket stitch hearts in place. Cross-stitch a button in center of each heart with red floss.

4 Pin peach teapot to cranberry teapot. Use red floss to backstitch horizontal lines at base and lid on peach teapot, stitching through both layers. Use ecru floss to work vertical straight stitches at base and lid of peach teapot; blanket stitch peach teapot to cranberry teapot. Pin teapots to antique white scalloped circle. Use blue floss to blanket stitch teapots in place. Remove any unwanted marker with cold water.

5 Center antique white scalloped circle over smaller hoop. Placing closure at top, press large hoop in place. Turn hoop to back, and run a bead of glue along back of hoop edge. Position hoop on denim scalloped circle so that scallops offset antique white scallops. Place heavy book on hoop until glue dries.

6 Use red floss to blanket stitch antique white scalloped edge to denim. Use red floss to cross-stitch remaining buttons in every other denim scallop. Tie raffia bow around hoop closure. Glue magnets to back.

Enlarge pattern 125 percent.

Henrietta Witch

Henrietta is a nice witch, though she is ready to fly away to her Halloween haunts! She is sure to delight all your little ghosts and goblins.

WHAT YOU'LL NEED

¼ yard unbleached muslin

1 package tan dye

Cardboard or plastic

Water-erasable marker

Scissors

Fabric marking pencil

Sewing machine

Cream thread

10 ounces polyester fiberfill

Pins

¼ yard each black, brown-
and-black check,
brown plaid fabrics

Iron, ironing board

2 black seed beads

10 inches red embroidery floss

Embroidery needle

Blusher

1 ounce wool roving for hair

White craft glue

½ yard black ribbon, ⅛ inch wide

1½×4-inch piece
gold-brown fabric

9-inch wooden meat skewer

1 Wash and dry muslin; do not use fabric softener. Following manufacturer's directions, dye muslin in sink. Let dry.

2 Trace and cut out all pattern pieces (on pages 56–57) on cardboard or plastic. Leg-shoe is 1 piece, and seam line is marked.

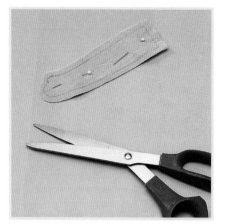

3 With muslin folded (9×22 inches), trace arms and head-body, leaving ½ inch between pieces. Traced lines are seam lines. For all pieces, cut ¼ inch away from all seam lines.

4 Sew 2 arm pieces together, leaving end open. Repeat with other arm pieces. Clip curves, and turn right side out. Stuff to 1 inch below ends. Baste tops closed.

5 Stitch from A to B around head. Pin arms in place at sides. Stitch sides, catching arms in seams. Clip curves, and turn right side out.

6 Cut 2½×15-inch piece from black; cut 9×15-inch piece from muslin. Stitch pieces together along 15-inch side, and press seam toward black fabric. On wrong side of doubled fabric, trace leg-shoe twice, lining up seam line on pattern with seam. (Remember to leave ½ inch between pieces.) Cut out leg-shoe ¼ inch from traced lines.

7 Stitch around 2 leg-shoe pieces on traced lines, leaving top open. Repeat for other leg-shoe pieces. Clip curves, and turn right side out. Stuff to 1½ inches below tops. Place seams side by side, and baste across the tops.

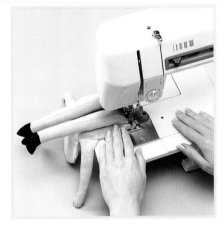

8 Stitch legs to front body at opening, making sure feet are facing forward. Stuff head and body, and stitch opening closed.

9 Pinch face together to form nose, and sew 2 stitches through pinched fabric and fiberfill. Sew on seed beads for eyes. With red floss, embroider mouth. Using finger, put blusher on cheeks.

10 Trace and cut out dress and sleeves from check fabric, vest from plaid, and hat from black. Note: For vest, cut out 1 back on doubled fabric, placing pattern on fold where indicated and cutting neck back as indicated. Then cut out fronts on doubled fabric, but cut along fold line (not ¼ inch away from line). Be sure to cut neck front where indicated.

11 Stitch dress at shoulder seams, and stitch sleeves to dress. Fringe bottom of sleeves by cutting slits 1 inch deep and ¼ inch apart. Stitch sleeve and side seams. Fringe bottom of dress in the same manner as sleeves. Hem neck opening. Place dress on doll. Sew a running stitch around neck to gather; knot thread. Above sleeve fringe, sew a running stitch above fringe to gather; knot thread. Repeat for other arm.

12 Hem vest armholes, neck, front, and bottom. Stitch shoulder seams. Place vest on doll.

13 Using craft glue, glue wool roving on doll for hair. Use fingers to lightly comb hair. Stitch back seam on hat, and turn right side out. Turn brim of hat up in front, and glue in place. Glue hat on doll's head. Tie black ribbon into a bow, and glue to front neck of dress.

14 Fringe gold-brown fabric in same manner as sleeves. Place glue on unfringed end of fabric, and roll fabric around end of meat skewer. Let dry. Stitch broom to 1 hand at thumb.

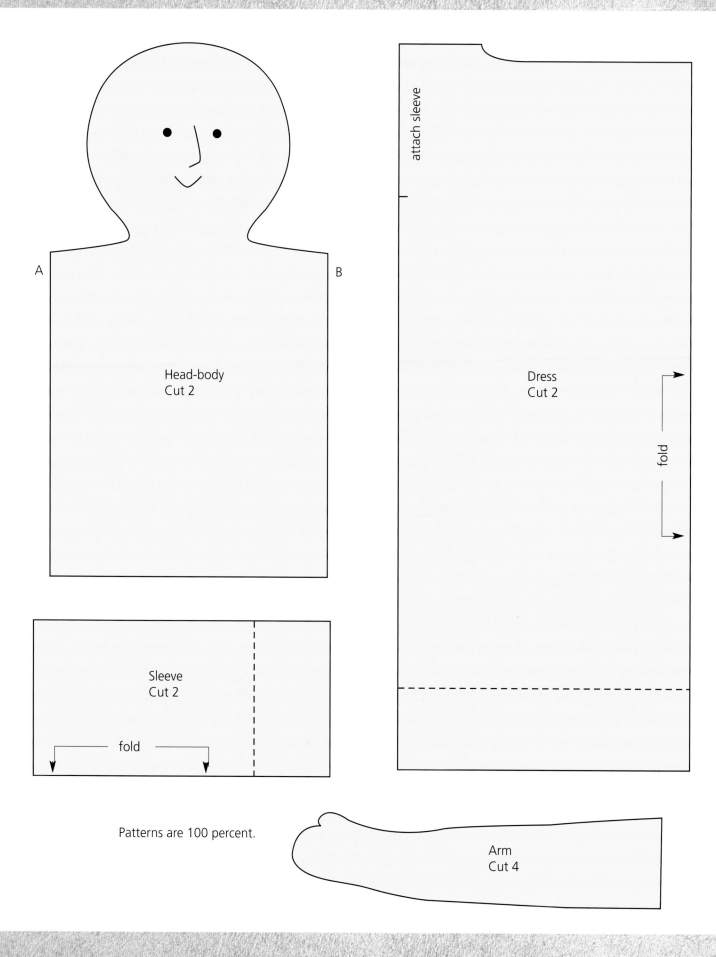

Head-body
Cut 2

A

B

Dress
Cut 2

attach sleeve

fold

Sleeve
Cut 2

fold

Patterns are 100 percent.

Arm
Cut 4

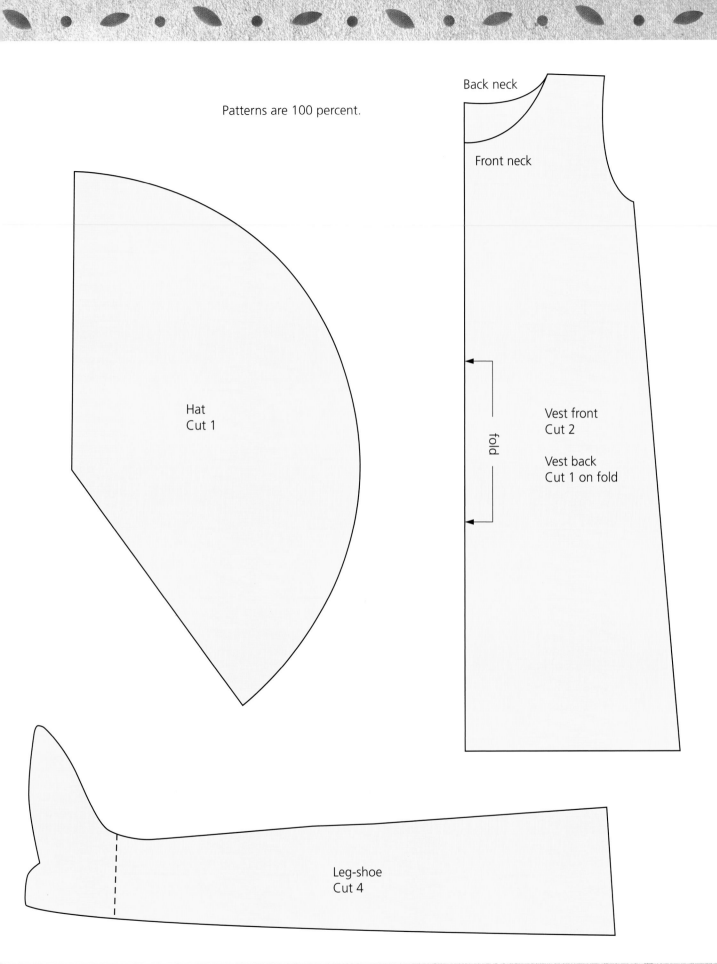

Patterns are 100 percent.

Back neck

Front neck

Hat
Cut 1

Vest front
Cut 2

Vest back
Cut 1 on fold

fold

Leg-shoe
Cut 4

Burlap Apple Bag

This apple bag is perfect for a casual centerpiece filled with apples. Or fill the bag with delicious muffins for a hostess gift!

WHAT YOU'LL NEED

Burlap cross-stitch bag
Embroidery floss (see color key)
Embroidery needle`

Colors	DMC
Light green	367
Dark green	319
Cream	746
Tan	677
Light red	221
Medium red	204
Dark red	349
Blue	312

1 Do all stitching with 6 strands of floss. Follow design around the bag, repeating design as necessary.

2 If you can't find a premade bag, make one. Cross-stitch pattern at top of fabric, leaving fabric unstitched at bottom. When you have cross-stitched length you want, sew cross-stitch fabric to top of coordinating fabric (right sides together). Fold over fabric to create bag lining. Sew sides and bottom of bag with right sides together, making sure to sew sides and bottom of cross-stitch fabric in seams.

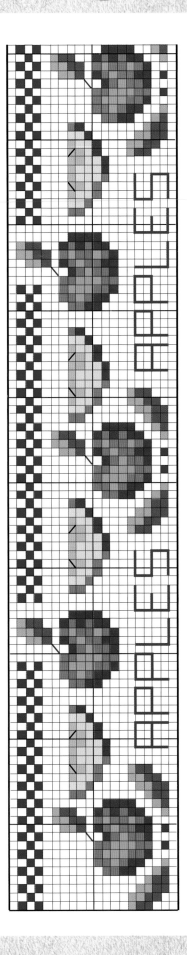

Fall Harvest Wreath

A feast for the eyes, this wreath is embellished with grapes, pomegranates, hydrangeas, zinnias, and ivy. The rich and deep fall colors will add an inviting warmth to your home.

WHAT YOU'LL NEED

18-inch grapevine wreath

6 stems silk green grape ivy

3 stems silk reddish-brown grape ivy, each with 2 bunches of grapes

Hot glue gun, glue sticks

3 to 4 dried pomegranates

10 to 12 dried assorted zinnia and black-eyed Susan heads

8 stems dried green hydrangeas

Wire cutters

1 Hot glue green and reddish-brown grape ivy around grapevine wreath.

2 Hot glue pomegranates and flower heads randomly around wreath in a circular design.

3 Hot glue hydrangea stems into the open areas of the grapevine wreath following the circular contour of wreath.

Tip

Try using dried mini corn or dried gourds on your fall harvest wreath. Sprinkle some cinnamon scented oils onto the wreath to add a special autumn fragrance.

Amber Lee

This delightfully versatile country doll can be decorated to represent any special occasion.

WHAT YOU'LL NEED

¼ yard unbleached muslin

1 package tan dye

Pencil

Cardboard or plastic

Scissors

Tape measure

Sewing machine

Tan thread

6 ounces polyester fiberfill

Pins

2×14-inch piece black fabric

5×14-inch piece red and tan
 stripe fabric

Iron, ironing board

1 ounce brown yarn, 4 ply

Sewing needle, thread

1 yard blue ribbon, ⅛ inch wide

Felt-tip fabric markers: black, red

Blusher

½ yard blue plaid fabric

4½×10-inch piece osnaburg cloth

4×4-inch piece fusible webbing

2×2-inch piece each red, blue,
 and green print

2 yards black embroidery floss

5 buttons, ⁷⁄₁₆ inch each: 2 blue,
 1 burgundy, 1 red, 1 white

4 round hook-and-loop
 fasteners, ½ inch each

4×8-inch piece red plaid print

8×8-inch piece cotton batting

3×3-inch piece yellow print

2×8-inch piece blue print

3×8-inch piece red and white
 stripe print

1 Wash and dry unbleached muslin; do not use fabric softener. Following manufacturer's directions, dye muslin tan.

2 Trace pattern pieces (on pages 66–67) on cardboard or plastic; cut out. Leg-shoe is 1 piece, and seam line is marked.

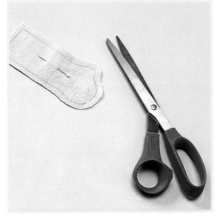

3 With muslin folded (9×22 inches), trace arm twice and head-body once, leaving at least ½ inch between pieces. Traced lines are seam lines. For all pieces, cut ¼ inch away from all seam lines.

4 Sew 2 arms together, leaving end open. Repeat with other arms. Clip curves, and turn right side out. Stuff to 1 inch below ends. Sew finger lines as marked on pattern. Baste ends closed.

5 Stitch from A to B around head. Pin arms in place at sides. Stitch sides, catching arms in seams. Clip curves, and turn right side out.

6 Stitch 2×14-inch black fabric to 5×14-inch red and tan stripe fabric along 14-inch edges. Press seam to black fabric. Fold fabric in half, right sides together, with seam lines matching. On wrong side of fabric trace leg-shoe twice, lining up seam line on pattern to seam of fabric (leave at least ½ inch between pieces). Cut out leg-shoe ¼ inch from traced lines.

7 Stitch around 2 leg-shoe pieces on traced lines, leaving top open. Repeat for other leg-shoe pieces. Clip curves, and turn right side out. Stuff to 1 inch below tops. Place seams side by side, and baste across top of both legs.

8 Stitch legs to front body at opening, making sure feet are facing forward. Stuff head and body, and stitch opening closed.

9 Cut yarn into 14-inch lengths. Stitch middle of each yarn strand to head at seam line. Stitch hair to front and back of head along stitching lines. Cut ribbon in half, and tie hair into ponytails. Trim hair.

10 Paint eyes and mouth on face with fabric markers. Use finger to add blusher to cheeks.

11 To make dress: Cut dress bodice front and back and skirt (5½×20 inches) from blue plaid. Cut apron (4½×10 inches) from osnaburg cloth.

12 Stitch dress bodice front and back at sleeves and sides.

13 Hem apron sides and bottom. Center apron on skirt, and baste along top. Gather skirt and apron, and stitch to dress bodice. Stitch dress back ½ inch above waist to bottom of skirt.

14 Hem bottom of skirt, edge of sleeves, neck, and back opening.

15 Following manufacturer's directions, press fusible webbing to back of 2-inch squares of red and blue print fabrics. Trace and cut out small hearts. Peel off paper backing, and press hearts to apron. Using black floss, blanket-stitch around hearts.

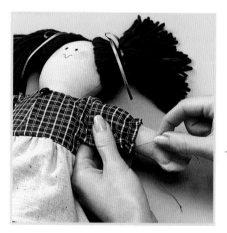

16 Put dress on doll. Stitch dress closed at neck back, and stitch blue button over stitches. Take a tuck at center of neck front, and stitch burgundy button at tuck. Gather sleeves around arms with a running stitch.

17 Stitch ½-inch round hook end of hook-and-loop fastener to right hand.

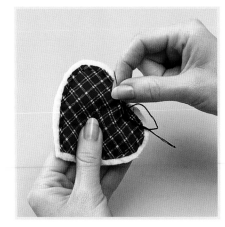

18 To make heart: Cut 2 red plaid hearts. Cut out 1 batting heart. Layer fabric hearts, right sides out, with batting between. Using black embroidery floss, stitch around outside with a running stitch, through all layers.

19 Cut out yellow fabric yo-yo circle and a green fabric leaf. Stitch around outside of circle, turning edge under ½ inch as you stitch. Pull thread to gather.

20 Stitch leaf and yo-yo flower to heart. Stitch ½-inch round loop end of hook-and-loop fastener to back of heart.

21 To make heart flag: Stitch 2×8-inch blue fabric to 3×8-inch red and white stripe.

22 Trace heart on wrong side of fabric, lining up seam line with seam. Fold fabric in half, right sides together. Layer 4-inch piece batting under 2 layers of fabric.

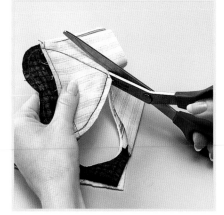

23 Stitch all the way around heart. Trim off excess fabric and batting. Clip curves and points. Take out enough stitches at side of seam of blue print fabric to turn. Turn right side out, and stitch opening closed.

24 Stitch red, white, and blue buttons to front of heart flag. Stitch ½-inch round loop end of hook-and-loop fastener to back of heart flag.

25 Use the same techniques to make a Christmas tree or Easter bunny. You can even make something special for Amber Lee to hold on Father's Day, Mother's Day, or an extra-special birthday!

Enlarge patterns 125 percent.

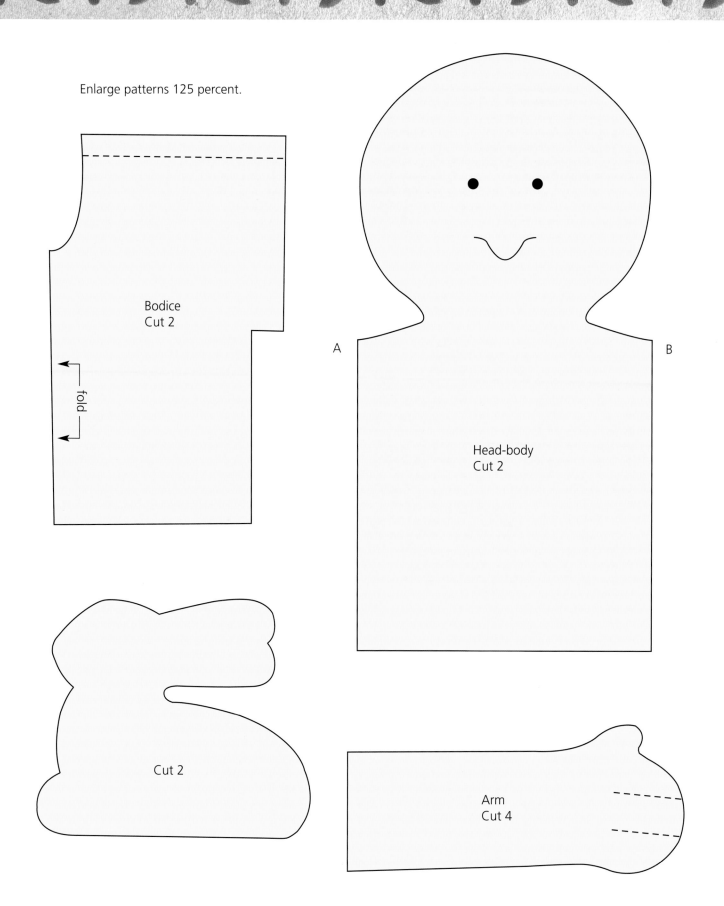

Bodice
Cut 2

fold

A

B

Head-body
Cut 2

Cut 2

Arm
Cut 4

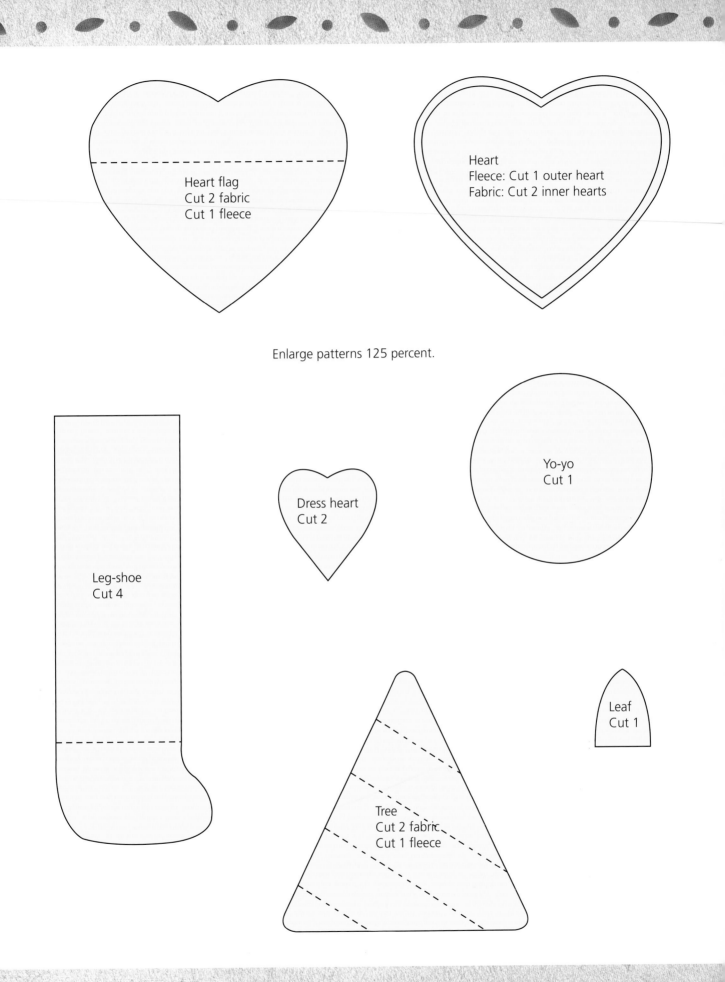

Heart flag
Cut 2 fabric
Cut 1 fleece

Heart
Fleece: Cut 1 outer heart
Fabric: Cut 2 inner hearts

Enlarge patterns 125 percent.

Leg-shoe
Cut 4

Dress heart
Cut 2

Yo-yo
Cut 1

Leaf
Cut 1

Tree
Cut 2 fabric
Cut 1 fleece

Stamped Recipe Cards

These cards make a terrific gift for anyone who cooks,

but you may want to make them just for yourself!

WHAT YOU'LL NEED

Tracing paper
Soft-lead pencil
Eraser carving material
Cutting surface or board
Craft knife (#11 blade)
Linoleum cutter (#21 blade)
Ink pads: red, yellow
Scrap paper
12 smooth off-white cards,
   4×6 inches each
Ruler
Dark green colored pencil
24-inch length dark green raffia

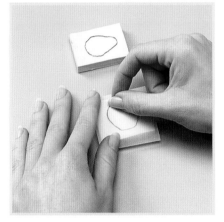

1 Trace pear and apple patterns below, using the pencil, and then transfer them to eraser carving material by placing paper facedown and rubbing back of image with your thumbnail.

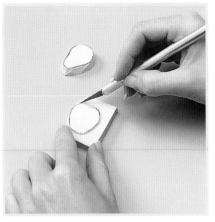

2 On cutting surface, cut 2 images apart with craft knife, and then cut them out using linoleum cutter. (As you cut, turn carving material rather than moving cutter.) Trim away excess from images with craft knife, slanting cuts away from image.

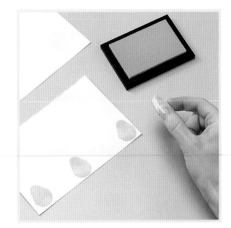

3 Using red and yellow ink pads, test images by stamping on scrap paper. Trim images if necessary.

4 On each card, stamp pear in yellow at each end and in middle along bottom. Stamp a red apple between pears.

5 Use ruler and dark green pencil to mark off lines ½ inch apart on each card, starting ½ inch from top. If desired, mark off lines on reverse side, as well. Use green pencil to draw in stems and leaves.

6 Bundle cards, and tie with raffia.

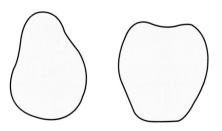

Patterns are 100 percent.

Tommy the Turkey

Tommy the Turkey will grace your Thanksgiving table. His whimsical face and colorful tail feathers make him a fine dinner companion.

2 With wrong sides together, stitch tail feathers together on traced lines, leaving opening to turn. Repeat with head-body. Clip curves and points, and turn.

3 Following manufacturer's directions, iron fusible webbing to backs of red and yellow fabrics.

4 Trace beak and wattle on paper of fusible webbing. Cut out pieces, and remove paper backing. Following manufacturer's directions, fuse beak and wattle to turkey face. Sew on buttons for eyes.

1 Trace or photocopy patterns on page 72. Trace turkey head-body on wrong side of brown fabric, trace tail feathers on wrong side of fall print. Traced lines are seam lines. Cut out ¼ inch outside drawn lines.

5 Stitch lines for tail feathers through both layers.

6 Stuff tail feathers and head-body. Stitch openings closed.

7 Using hot glue gun, glue tail feathers to head-body.

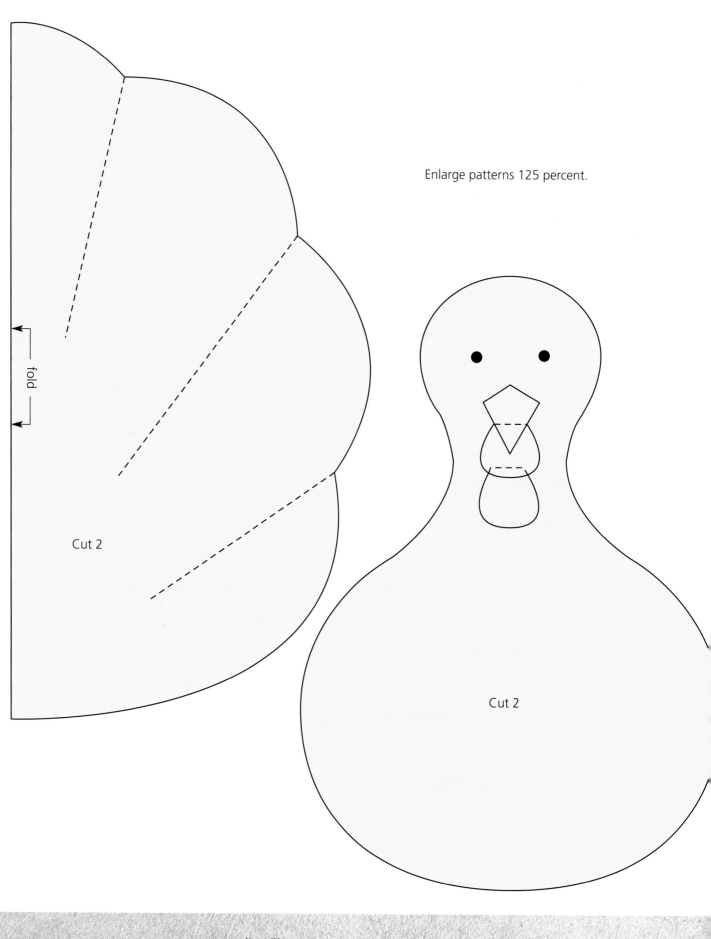

fold

Cut 2

Enlarge patterns 125 percent.

Cut 2

Halloween Delights

Your favorite kid is going to love this special,

sturdy bag for holding all those Halloween treats!

1 Cut two 17×12-inch pieces of fusible webbing. From the Halloween fabrics cut a 12×5-inch piece, 4⅛×7-inch piece, 8×7-inch piece, and 5×12-inch piece. Cut 17×12-inch piece fabric for bag back.

2 Lay fabric sections for bag front onto one 17×12-inch piece of fusible webbing, and fuse according to manufacturer's directions. Adhere back fabric to other piece of fusible webbing. Remove paper backing. Bond to front and back of bag.

3 Iron fusible webbing to black scrap fabric for cutouts. Trace and cut pattern pieces on page 75 from desired fabrics. Remove paper backing.

4 Arrange cutouts on bag front using picture as guide. Press in place. With permanent marker, write "Trick or Treat" on moon.

5 Cover entire bag with vinyl. To determine amount, measure bag starting at top of bag front, down under bag bottom, and back up to top of bag back; add 1 inch to this measurement. Cut measured amount.

6 Center bag bottom on center of paper side of vinyl. Vinyl will be wider than bag; excess will aid in covering bag sides. Mark bag bottom corners on paper backing. Cut vinyl to mark from each edge.

7 Remove paper backing to first set of cuts. Lay bag front onto sticky side of vinyl. Hand-press in place. Fold excess vinyl onto sides of bag. Continue to remove paper backing to next set of cuts. Hand-press bag bottom in place, leaving excess on sides alone. Remove remaining paper backing, hand-press to bag back and fold excess to bag sides. Fold bottom excess up onto bag sides. Fold any excess at top of bag to inside, making cuts at handles for proper fit. Iron according to manufacturer's directions. Cut pieces of vinyl to fit uncovered bag area on sides. Bond following manufacturer's directions.

Enlarge patterns 125 percent.

Cranberry Cedar Wreath

This stunning holiday wreath will convey a warm welcome to your home.

WHAT YOU'LL NEED

5 stems preserved cedar

3 stems preserved fir

Wire cutters

Hot glue gun, glue sticks

15-inch birch wreath

22-gauge floral wire

4 to 5 pinecones

4 to 5 stems silk red cranberries, each with 2 bunches of berries and 1 bud

1 yard red and green cloth Christmas ribbon

2 Cut a long length of wire for each pinecone. Wrap a piece of wire around bottom of a pinecone. Repeat for all pinecones. Attach cones to wreath using wire.

3 Cut cranberry stems 10 to 15 inches long, and hot glue stems in a circular pattern around center of wreath.

4 Make a 2-loop bow. Use wire to attach bow to right side of wreath.

1 Cut cedar and fir 10 to 18 inches long. Hot glue pieces in a circular pattern around wreath following lines of extending branches.

Winter Wonderland Birdhouse

Bring a touch of winter charm into your home

with this decorative birdhouse.

WHAT YOU'LL NEED

3 pieces wood
   (1×12×11½ inches for base;
   2×4×3½ inches and
   1×4×3½ inches for pole
   supports)

Sandpaper

Tack cloth

Drill, 1-inch wood drill bit

Large birdhouse

1-inch wood dowel, 3 feet long

Acrylic paint: burnt umber,
   snow white, country red

1-inch paintbrush

Crackle medium

Hot glue gun, glue sticks

Wood glue

Matte finishing spray

Pine garland

4 silk holly sprigs with berries

Decorative cardinal

1 Sand rough edges of wood, and tack. Drill 1-inch holes through middle of 2 pole supports. If possible, remove perch. Basecoat birdhouse, perch, and bottom base burnt umber. Basecoat pole (dowel) snow white. Basecoat pole supports country red. Let all pieces dry.

2 Apply crackle medium (following manufacturer's directions) on birdhouse, perch, and bottom base. Let dry completely.

3 Paint birdhouse walls snow white. Let dry completely. Paint roof, eaves, bottom of birdhouse, perch, and base country red. Let dry completely.

4 Glue 1-inch support to center bottom of birdhouse with glue gun. Glue 2-inch support to center top of base, and let dry. Insert pole into holes in supports, and line up house and base so they are square. Glue pole in place with wood glue. Glue perch in place.

5 Spray entirely with matte finishing spray, and let dry.

6 Attach pine garland end to base with hot glue. Twist garland up and around pole, gluing on back side of pole. Continue over side of house and drape over roof and around front corner of house.

7 Glue 3 holly sprigs along pole, 1 sprig on center peak of roof, and a few berries under perch. Glue cardinal to top of house.

Fuzzie Bear

Whether you make him as a gift for your favorite child or for yourself, this adorable bear cheers up anyone holding him!

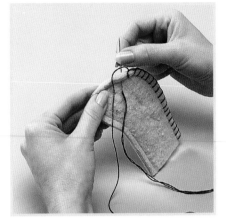

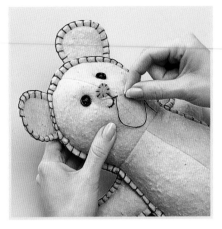

7 Stuff head and body section, and stitch opening closed. Blanket-stitch around head and body.

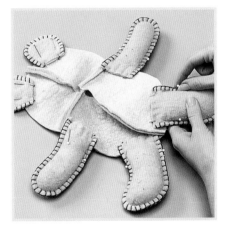

1 Following manufacturer's directions, wash and dry batting. Following manufacturer's directions, dye batting tan in sink.

2 Trace all pattern pieces on page 82 on paper. Fold batting in half, right sides together. Pin and cut out all pattern pieces on 2 layers of batting. (Note: Cut out all pieces ¼ inch from lines; drawn lines are seam lines.)

3 With right sides together, stitch head front seam, head back seam, body front seam, and body back seam. Clip curves.

4 With right sides together, stitch front head to front body at neck. Stitch back head to back body at neck, leaving open space to stuff where marked.

5 All remaining seams are stitched wrong side to wrong side, so raw edges will be exposed. Stitch legs, arms, and ears, leaving open to stuff where marked. Using brown cotton, blanket-stitch around seamed edges. Stuff legs and arms to 1 inch below top. Baste openings closed.

6 Pin ears to wrong side of back of head, and pin legs and arms to wrong side of body section. Place front head and body section on back section, wrong sides together. Pin in place, and stitch around head and body sections.

8 Use brown embroidery floss to stitch buttons on for eyes. Stitch on nose and embroider mouth with brown floss.

9 Fold 2½×36-inch blue fabric in half to measure 1¼×36 inches. Stitch ends and sides, leaving an opening in the middle to turn. Turn, and stitch opening closed. Tie in a bow at the neck of the bear.

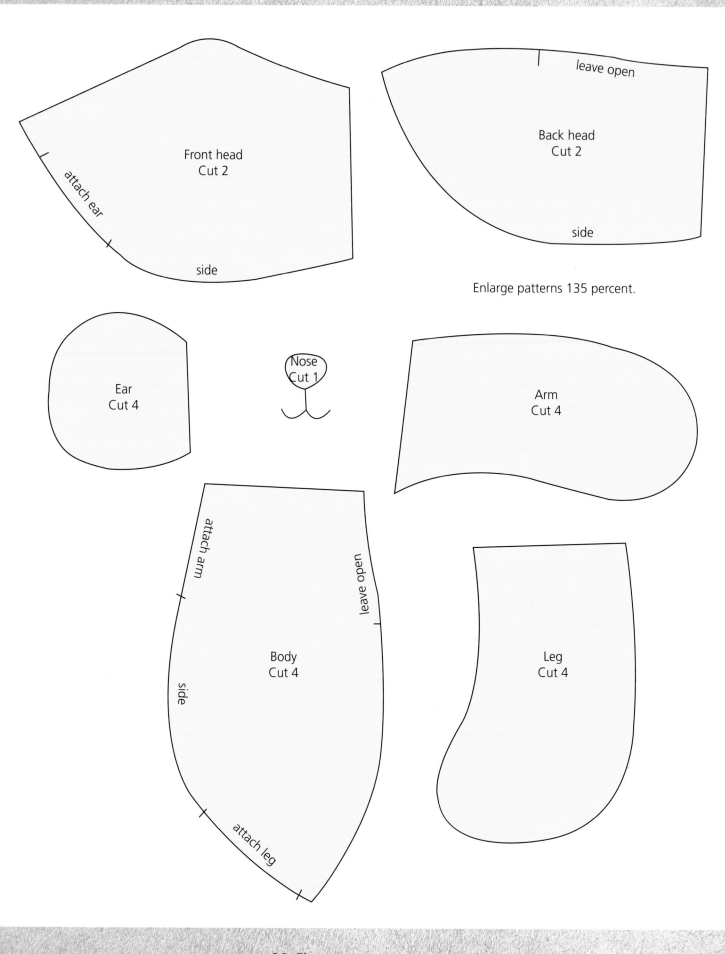

Front head
Cut 2

attach ear

side

Back head
Cut 2

leave open

side

Enlarge patterns 135 percent.

Ear
Cut 4

Nose
Cut 1

Arm
Cut 4

attach arm

leave open

Body
Cut 4

side

attach leg

Leg
Cut 4

Country Folk Santa

This folk art Santa is sure to fly into your heart

and become part of your family holiday traditions.

WHAT YOU'LL NEED

- 1-inch pine board
- Stylus
- Graphite paper
- Jigsaw
- Sandpaper
- Tack cloth
- Drill, small drill bit
- Waterbase varnish
- Acrylic paint: buttermilk, ebony black, country red, green meadow
- Paintbrushes: small flat, 10/0 liner, spatter tool
- Jute twine
- Scissors
- Craft glue

1 Apply patterns on page 85 to wood using stylus and graphite paper.

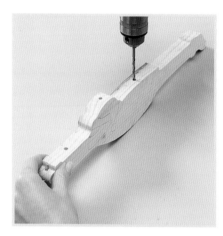

2 Cut out Santa and bag. Sand until smooth, and tack. Drill 2 holes through the thickness of the wood: 1 in top of hands and second approximately 1½ inches closer to the head. Make sure holes are completely through. Drill holes through bag, the same distance apart as holes in arms. Drill two ¼-inch-deep holes on the top edge of Santa, 1 at top of head and the other in front of waist.

3 Mix varnish and acrylic paint to make a stain. Test on wood scrap for proper transparency. Wrap color around edge (thickness) of wood. Leave Santa's face bare. Fur, beard, and candy cane are buttermilk. Belt and boots are ebony black. Suit, ball in bag, and candy cane stripe are country red. Gloves and bag are green meadow. Let dry.

4 Line entire pattern with ebony black.

5 Spatter front and thicknesses of wood with ebony black. Let dry.

6 Varnish all pieces. Let dry.

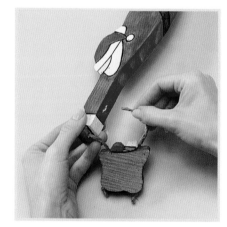

7 Cut two 4-inch pieces of jute twine. Tie a knot in 1 end of twine. Thread other end of twine from bottom of bag through drilled hole. Thread same piece through arm; tie a knot in end. Repeat with second piece of twine through other hole in bag and in Santa's arm. For hanger, cut a 12-inch piece of twine. Tie a tight bow in center of twine. Insert glue in shallow drilled holes, and push twine ends in holes. Let dry.

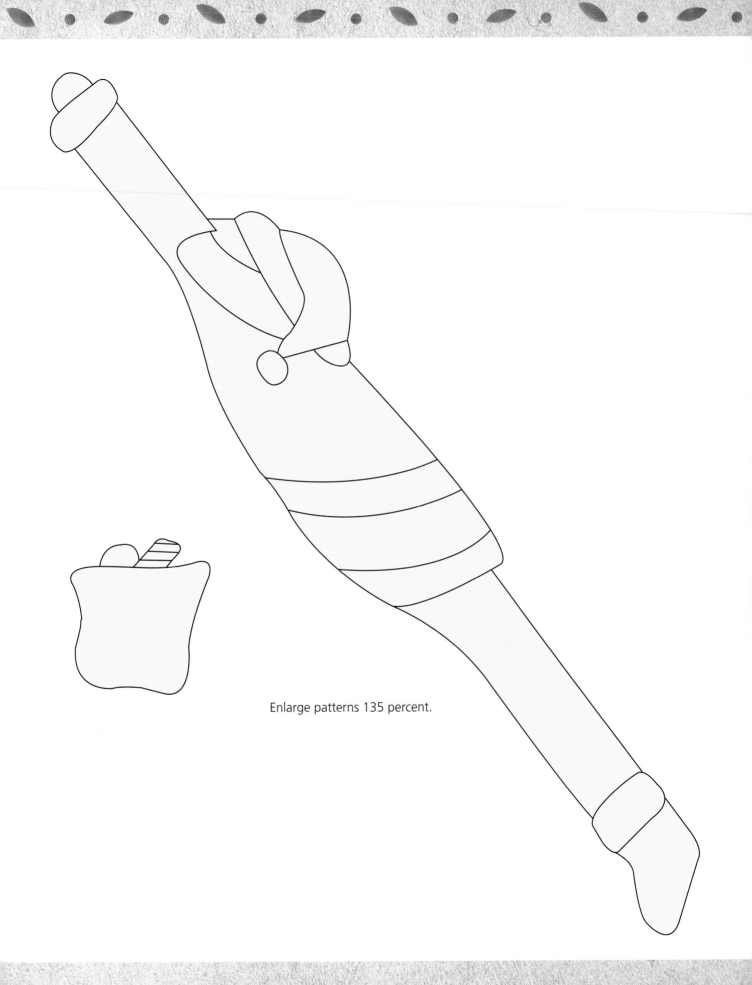

Enlarge patterns 135 percent.

Southern Magnolia Holiday

The South's most beautiful flower is highlighted on this holiday wreath. Ivory magnolias dance through Christmas greenery, glass ornaments, and golden holly leaves.

WHAT YOU'LL NEED

5 silk magnolias with 4 buds

Wire cutters

Floral wire

Artificial pine wreath

Hot glue gun, glue sticks

27 gold glass ball ornaments on wire picks, 1 inch each

2 gold silk holly branches

72 inches sheer wired ribbon

10 natural pinecones

2 Insert magnolias and buds into wreath. Twist pine branches around stems to secure. Add a touch of hot glue for extra security. Space flowers evenly around wreath, leaving room for ornaments.

5 Cut ribbon into three 24-inch pieces. Form 2 loops of ribbon, and twist together with floral wire. Secure each ribbon to wreath behind a magnolia. Keep ribbon loops to sides of flowers so flowers remain dominant. Space ribbons evenly around wreath.

6 Glue in pinecones and any remaining holly leaves to hide any glue or wire.

1 Cut stems of magnolia flowers to 2 inches. Cut off buds and leaves from stems. Form a collar around flower with leaves, and wrap with floral wire to hold in place. Repeat for all flowers and buds.

3 Twist 2 glass ball stems together to form a cluster. Make 9 clusters. In the same way, make 3 clusters with 3 balls. Insert clusters into wreath between magnolias. Twist pine branches around clusters to hold them in place.

4 Cut holly branches into 3- to 4-inch pieces. Glue them into wreath around magnolias. Glue remaining magnolia leaves to hide any wire that shows.

Variation

The gold and ivory color combination of this wreath can be changed to suit your home decor. Consider using red, green, or even blue ornaments to complement the classic ivory magnolias. Red and green trim would give the wreath a more traditional appeal for the holiday season.

Happy Holiday Vest

If you've been looking for that special outfit to wear to a holiday party, why not make it yourself? This vest can be made in one day for a weekend gathering.

WHAT YOU'LL NEED

1½×22-inch strip each red and gold print fabrics

Sewing machine, sewing needle

Thread: black, white, yellow, brown, dark gold

Ruler

Scissors

9×14-inch piece each green print and off-white print fabrics

14×15½-inch piece beige print

10×11-inch piece green print

9×14-inch piece gold print

14×14½-inch piece blue print

Your favorite vest pattern

½ yard fusible webbing

Appliqué fabric pieces: 8×8-inch white on white, 7×7-inch red print, 4×4-inch red print, 7×7-inch green print, 2×2-inch brown print, 2×2-inch yellow print, 2×2-inch black print, 4×4-inch gold print, 3×3-inch brown print

Iron, ironing board

8 black seed beads

6 buttons, various colors and sizes

1½ yards lining and back fabric

3 buttons, ¾ inch each

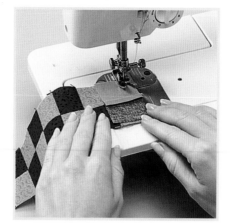

1 To make checked piece: Stitch 1½-inch strip red print to 1½-inch strip gold print along 22-inch length. Cut into fourteen 1½-inch-wide pieces. Stitch sections together, alternating colors.

2 To make pinwheel section: Cut 12 triangles (see pattern) from green print and 12 from off-white print (dashed line is stitching line). Stitch a green triangle to an off-white triangle on the diagonal to form a square. Repeat for all triangles (make 12 squares).

3 Stitch 4 squares together to create a pinwheel. Stitch pinwheel blocks together to make a row.

4 To make right vest front: Stitch checked piece to top of 14×15½-inch beige print.

5 Stitch 10×11-inch green print to top of checked piece, lining up pieces along left edge. Cut out right front of vest.

6 To make left front: Stitch pinwheel section to top of 9×14-inch gold print.

7 Stitch 14×14½-inch blue print to top of pinwheel section, lining up pieces along right edge. Cut out left front of vest.

8 To make appliqués: Following manufacturer's directions, iron fusible webbing to back of all appliqué fabrics. Trace appliqué patterns onto paper backing, and cut out all pieces.

9 Peel off paper from all pieces, and place on vest fronts, following finished photo for placement. Iron in place.

10 Using blanket stitch on sewing machine, appliqué all pieces on vest fronts. Use thread colors as follows: black for tree, mitten, hat, house; white for mitten cuff, snowman, snow; yellow for window; brown for door, trunk; and dark gold for star, scarf. Knot all threads on back of fabric.

11 Stitch beads to snowman for eyes, nose, and mouth. Stitch buttons to snowman, star, and door at Xs.

12 Cut out remaining vest pieces, and assemble vest following pattern directions. Sew on ¾-inch buttons.

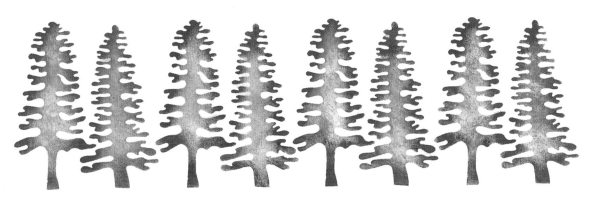

Enlarge patterns 150 percent.

Snoozing Bear and Starlight Can Covers

Use these adorable cans as gift containers. But don't count

on the bears to guard what's inside—one's a real snoozer!

WHAT YOU'LL NEED

2 large cans, about 7 inches tall and 6 inches in diameter

18×42 inches royal blue felt

Ruler

Scissors

Fabric marking pencil

1⅓ yards fusible webbing

10×14 inches dark heather brown plush felt

¼ yard hunter green plush felt

4×6 inches heather gray plush felt

8×11 inches gold felt

Iron, ironing board

Black persian wool (or embroidery floss)

Embroidery needle

Tacky craft glue

Clothespins

Press cloth (optional)

1 Remove labels, wash cans, and check tops for sharp edges. (Hint: Use label to determine size to cut background.) Cut background royal blue felt 1 inch taller and ½ inch longer than cans.

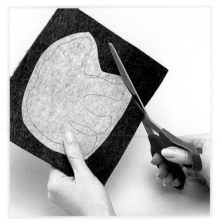

2 Trace bears, ground patterns, tree trunk, treetop, and 16 stars (patterns on page 94) onto paper side of fusible webbing. (Ground patterns are repeated around can.) Fuse bears to dark heather brown, ground patterns and treetop to hunter green, tree trunk to heather gray, and stars to gold felt. (Hint: Test felt scrap with iron before fusing. If iron drags, use a press cloth and steam to set fusible webbing.) Cut out all appliqués.

3 Referring to photos, fuse appliqués to backgrounds.

4 Using 1 strand of persian wool, work a blanket stitch across top edge of ground and around tree. Use short straight stitches to suggest blanket stitch around stars. For bears, embroider noses with wool. Outline eyelashes, ears, and claws with long straight stitches. For snoozing bear, sew a straight stitch as shown by dotted lines on pattern to define bear's arms and legs.

5 Glue appliquéd backgrounds to cans, overlapping where ends join and leaving 1 inch above can tops. Fold and glue 1 inch over top edge to inside. (Hint: Use clothespins to hold until glue sets.)

Enlarge patterns 150 percent.

Starlight ground pattern

Snoozing ground pattern

Country Home Decorating

Contents

For crafting information and instructions,
see Craft Techniques on pages 4–17.

Pansied Pressed Flowers

With these pressed flowers hanging in your kitchen,
you'll be reminded that spring is just around the corner!

What You'll Need

🌿

- 3 pansies
- Fern leaves
- Waxed paper
- Cardboard
- Heavy book
- Two 5×7-inch sheets of glass, ⅛ inch thick (have glass shop drill ⅛-inch holes at top corners of glass)
- Glass cleaner
- Lint-free cloth
- Adhesive copper foil, ½ inch wide
- Ruler
- Scissors
- Copper wire: 24 and 14 gauge
- Wire cutters
- Cotton gloves (optional)

2 Lay glass on a smooth, dry surface. Clean both sides well with glass cleaner and lint-free cloth. (Wear clean cotton gloves to eliminate fingerprints.) Arrange flowers and ferns on a sheet of glass, placing materials about ¼ inch inside outer edge of glass. Carefully place second sheet of glass on top of first.

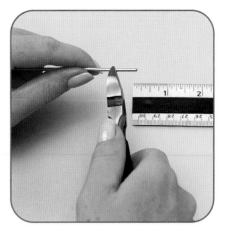

4 Cut a 10-inch piece of 24-gauge copper wire. Cut two ½-inch pieces of 14-gauge copper wire for pins.

5 To attach copper hanging wire, insert 10-inch length through both holes from back. Wrap each end of wire tightly around a copper pin to anchor wire in place.

1 Arrange pansies and ferns on waxed paper, and cover with a second sheet of waxed paper. Place a piece of cardboard on top. Place layers between pages of a heavy book. Leave book in a warm, dry place for 4 to 6 weeks.

3 Cut a long strip of copper foil ½ inch longer than total length of all sides of glass. Peel off paper backing, and center strip along edge of glass. Be sure there is the same amount of copper foil on each side of glass. Press lightly, and fold both sides of foil onto glass to adhere. Fold short ends over and around corners. Repeat on all sides.

Sunflower Delight

Extend the warm colors of rustic country fields with this mixture of yellow sunflowers, orange pumpkins, and burgundy Indian corn.

What You'll Need
🌿

3½×6½×6½-inch distressed wood crate

3×4×4-inch block dry floral foam

Hot glue gun, glue sticks

Sheet moss

2 to 4 pieces green reindeer moss

2 stems mustard yellow silk sunflowers, with 4- to 5-inch heads each

Wire cutters

Mustard yellow silk sunflower spray, with two 2-inch heads and 1 bud

Sunflower seed packet

3-inch silk pumpkin pick

Burgundy mini Indian corn

Metal garden spade

Dried black-eyed Susan head

6 to 8 branches green preserved eucalyptus

4 to 5 wood branches

4 to 5 strands natural raffia

Scissors

2 Using wire cutters, trim a large sunflower 21 to 22 inches long and insert into middle of crate. Cut second large sunflower 15 to 16 inches long and insert right of center. Cut a sunflower off the sunflower spray, and trim wire. Cut the spray 10 to 12 inches long, and insert it into left side of crate.

3 Hot glue the seed packet, trimmed sunflower, pumpkin pick, and Indian corn into base of crate.

4 Hot glue the end of the spade tip and insert into the foam at front left of crate. Hot glue black-eyed Susan to spade.

5 Cut eucalyptus 16 to 18 inches long and insert behind sunflowers. Cut shorter pieces of eucalyptus, and insert around sides of crate. Insert other branches throughout arrangement. Tie raffia to spade handle.

Tip
🌿

You can add a few drops of your favorite fall-scented oil to the moss to bring in the fragrance of the season.

1 Glue foam into crate. Cover foam with moss.

Lily Bud Quilt

You can grow some beautiful memories with this lily bud crib quilt. Let your talents blossom with this elegant design!

What You'll Need

Rotary cutter, self-healing mat

Quilt ruler

1⅜ yards white-on-cream fabric

⅜ yard light green calico fabric

¼ yard peach/green plaid fabric

¾ yard peach calico fabric

⅜ yard dark peach fabric

¼ yard dark green fabric

1¾ yards backing fabric

⅜ yard binding fabric

1½ yards light fusible webbing

1 package light fusible strip webbing, ⅜-inch roll

Iron, ironing board

45×60 inches low-loft polyester batting

1 package sea foam green singlefold bias tape

Pins

Sewing needle

Thread: dark green, peach

Notes

Quilt Dimensions: 39¼×54½

See Craft Techniques for quilting instructions on pages 13–17.

1 From white-on-cream, cut 21×36-inch rectangle and four 6×45-inch strips. Cut 2 strips to 6×40 inches and 2 strips to 6×35¾ inches. From light green, cut two 11-inch squares; cut squares on diagonal, forming 4 triangles.

2 Fuse 7×13-inch piece of webbing to plaid. Remove paper. Cut two 6-inch squares, and cut each on both diagonals, forming 8 triangles (discard 2).

3 From peach calico, cut nine 2½×45-inch strips. Cut 1 strip into two 21-inch pieces and 2 strips into 36-inch pieces. Cut 2 strips into 35¾-inch pieces and 4 strips into 24¾-inch pieces for outer border. Fuse four 2×17-inch pieces of webbing to 4 pieces of peach calico remaining from outer border. Remove paper, and cut into four 1½×17-inch strips.

4 Line up strips, 1 on top of the other, 2 right sides up and 2 right sides down. Place on horizontal line of cutting mat. Place 45 degree line of ruler on same line, and cut. Keeping same angle, move over 2⅛ inches, and cut. Cut 12 parallelograms.

5 From dark peach, cut two 2×45-inch strips and two 2½×45-inch strips. From 1 of the 2½-inch strips, cut ten 2½-inch squares. Cut 2½×15-inch piece from remainder. Cut other 2½-inch strip into three 15-inch pieces. Fuse 2½×15-inch piece of webbing to each of four 15-inch strips. Remove paper, and cut each strip to 2⅛×15 inches. Line up strips, 1 on top of the other, and place on horizontal line of cutting mat. Straighten edges. Cut at 2⅛-inch marking. Cut 20 squares.

6 From two 2×45-inch strips of dark peach, cut four 2×17-inch pieces. Cut four 2×17-inch pieces of webbing, and fuse to dark peach pieces. Remove paper, and cut each piece to 1½×17 inches. Follow step 4 to cut 12 parallelograms.

7 From dark green, cut four 2×45-inch strips. From webbing, cut ten 2×17-inch strips. Trim 8 webbing strips to 2×15 inches. Fuse two 2×17-inch pieces of webbing side by side to dark green strip. Using leaf pattern pieces, trace 4 large leaves and 16 small leaves. Cut out, and remove paper.

8 Cut each of 3 remaining dark green strips into three 2×15-inch pieces. Fuse 2×15-inch piece of webbing to 8 dark green pieces. Remove paper, and cut each of 8 strips to 1½×15 inches. Take 4 strips at a time and follow step 4, making 1-inch parallelograms. Make 40.

9 From both the bias tape and strip webbing, cut 2 pieces 11¼ inches long and 1 piece 23 inches long. Fuse webbing to tape, and remove paper.

10 Fuse strip webbing to long edge of each light green triangle. Remove paper. Place light green triangles on top of white-on-cream center rectangle at corners, match edges, and pin. Triangles will overlap slightly. Fuse triangles, and hand-baste layers together at edges.

11 Arrange 12 dark peach parallelograms (see photograph). Points are ¼ inch from side edges and just touch green triangles. Fuse. Place peach calico pieces to bottom sides of dark peach, and fuse. Outer pieces touch light green triangles.

12 Using ruler, fuse long piece of bias tape between top and bottom flowers. Fuse 2 shorter pieces of bias tape on straight line between side flowers. Center plaid triangles over bias tape, and line them up with rest of flower sections. Fuse. Place 4 large green leaves on a diagonal line, and fuse to center.

13 Pin and stitch 2½×36-inch peach calico strips to either side of center section. Press seams toward calico.

14 Stitch dark peach square (unfused) to both ends of 21-inch peach calico strips. Press seams toward squares. Matching seams of corner squares to side seams, pin and stitch to top and bottom.

15 With 6×40-inch strip of white-on-cream, line up 6 buds and 12 leaves on each strip (see photograph). Fuse pieces 1½ inches from each side and each end, leaving 2-inch space in the middle. Repeat. Pin and stitch strips to sides. With 6×35¾-inch strip of white-on-cream, center 4 buds and 8 leaves 1½ inches from top and bottom of each strip. Fuse. Center

small green leaves facing diagonally in 5¾-inch area on strip end, and fuse. Repeat with remaining 3 leaf sections. Pin and stitch strips to top and bottom.

16 Stitch two 24¾-inch peach calico strips on either side of dark peach square for outer border. Press seams toward squares. Pin and stitch long strips to each side of quilt, and press seams toward peach calico.

17 Stitch dark peach square to each end of two 35¾-inch peach calico strips. Press seams toward squares. Matching side seams with square seams, pin and stitch last strips to top and bottom of quilt. Press seams toward peach calico strips.

18 Place backing facedown, and center batting on top. Place quilt top faceup over batting. Pin, and hand-baste. Starting at center and using dark green thread, straight stitch bias tape stems on both edges of bias tape. Backstitch at beginning and end of each line of stitching. Change to medium zigzag stitch, and zigzag 4 dark green large leaf edges and long sides of corner triangles.

19 Using peach thread, zigzag stitch around all dark peach and peach calico parallelograms and plaid triangles in center section. Straight stitch around peach calico inner borders and squares. Zigzag dark peach buds around outside. With dark green thread, zigzag around bud leaves and corner diagonal leaf sections.

20 For binding, cut five 2×45-inch strips. Stitch strips together to make 1 long strip. Fold in half lengthwise, wrong sides together. Stitch binding to quilt top, beginning in middle of 1 side and leaving 3 inches of binding free. End stitching ¼ inch from each corner. Begin next side, and repeat for all sides and corners. End stitching about 6 inches before binding ends meet. Stitch ends of binding, trim excess, and finish stitching binding. Trim batting and backing. Miter corners, turn binding to back, and blind stitch in place. Remove basting.

Patterns are 100 percent.

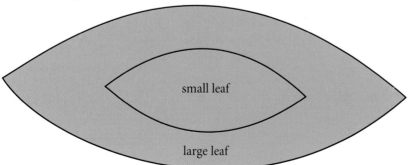

small leaf

large leaf

Spring Garden Sampler

A country cross-stitched sampler will add warmth to any room you hang it in. Personalize this sampler with your favorite gardening phrase!

What You'll Need

16×13-inch piece misty taupe cross-stitch cloth, 14 count

#24 tapestry needle

Embroidery floss (see color key)

Do all cross-stitch and names on seed packets with 2 strands of floss and all backstitch with 1 strand.

Colors	DMC #
Light green	368
Medium green	320
Dark green	319
Light yellow	727
Medium yellow	725
Gold	783
Light brown	435
Medium brown	433
Light pink	3713
Medium pink	605
Dark pink	961
Light purple	554
Dark purple	552
Light gray	415
White	414
Wildflowers	(variegated)

Notes

Overlap chart at arrows.

See Craft Techniques for cross-stitch instructions on pages 5–6.

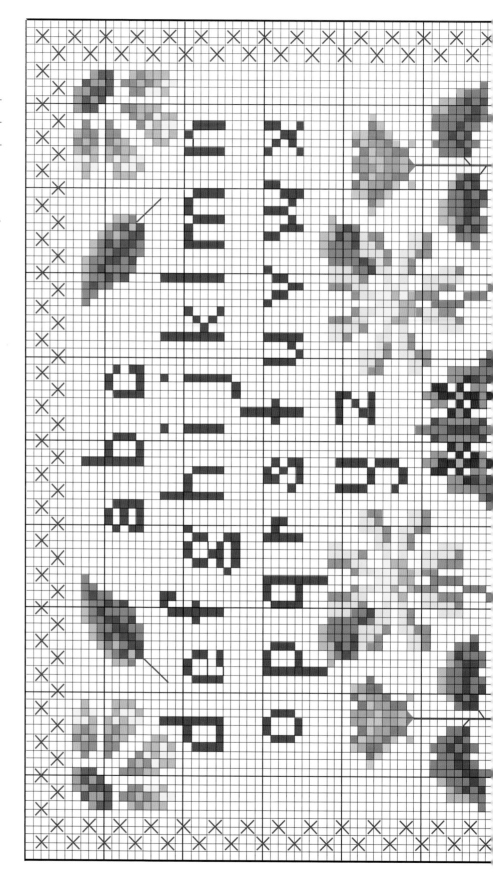

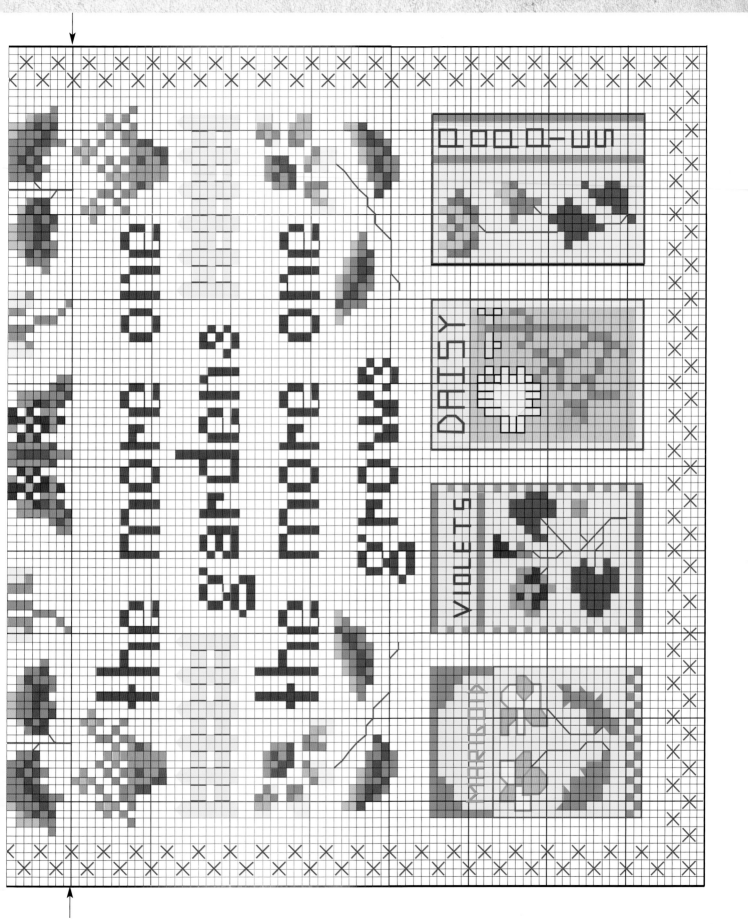

Rustic Rake and Garden Spade

Splendors of your garden are displayed in this colorful mixture of dried flowers, blooming bulbs, and country clay pots.

What You'll Need

3 terra-cotta pots: two 3-inch, one 2-inch

Acrylic paint: dark green, gold

Small sponge

10×27-inch wood rake

22-gauge floral wire

Wire cutters

Metal and wood handle garden spade

3×4×8-inch block dry floral foam

Serrated knife

Hot glue gun, glue sticks

Sheet moss

3 garden bulbs

Zinnia seed packet

10 to 12 stems fresh or dried pink statice

Dried purple zinnia head

8 stems yarrow

10 stems dried poppy pods

3 to 4 stems dried yellow heather

5 to 6 stems dried basil lepidium

3 to 4 stems dried green broom

1 or 2 stems fresh or dried lemon leaf (salal)

3 to 4 branches honeysuckle garland vine

1 Sponge paint clay pots green. Let dry. Lightly sponge pots gold over green paint. Let dry.

2 Wire clay pots to top center of rake. Wire spade to side top of rake.

3 Cut foam, and hot glue pieces inside and around clay pots. Hot glue moss to foam.

4 Hot glue 3 garden bulbs and seed packet onto garden spade. Cut and hot glue statice into clay pots and remaining dried and fresh flowers in and around clay pots and down the handle of the rake.

5 Glue honeysuckle vine throughout the design.

Magnolia Swag

Add silk magnolias to a grapevine swag, and greet your guests with the elegance of southern hospitality.

What You'll Need

- 18- to 24-inch grapevine swag
- 18-gauge wire
- Wire cutters
- 2½ yards gold mesh ribbon, 2 inches wide
- Scissors
- Fabric glue
- Thin wire
- Floral picks
- Florist tape
- Cool-temp glue gun, glue sticks
- 34-inch silk magnolia stem: 18 to 24 leaves, 1 bud, 2 flowers
- 3 to 5 vinyl pears, 3 inches each (picks attached)
- 16 to 24 dried eucalyptus stems, 12 inches each
- 4 to 8 stems assorted silk green leaves, 12 inches each
- 8 to 12 silk wheat stems with leaves, 18 inches each
- 8 to 12 silk baby's breath stems, 18 inches each

2 Make a 5-loop bow with tails on either side. Angle-cut ribbon ends, and seal edges with fabric glue. Secure ribbon with a thin wire. Attach to a floral pick; wrap pick with florist tape. Glue bow in center of swag. Attach tails with thin wire (or hot glue) along sides of swag.

4 Glue eucalyptus stems around outside edges of swag. Fill in spaces with assorted silk leaves.

5 Glue wheat stems and baby's breath radiating from center of swag.

3 Remove leaves and blossoms from magnolia stem. Attach flowers to floral picks; wrap with florist tape. Glue blossoms near bow, slightly to the right side of swag. Glue bud to left side of swag. Glue pears around swag in a pleasing manner.

1 Cut a length of wire about 8 inches long. To make a hanger, twist wire around a few branches on back of swag and make a loop.

Silk Ribbon Heart

Create this enchanting floral heart to hang in a room where you want that extra-special romantic touch.

What You'll Need

Plain white paper

#2 pencil

Tape

8½×7½-inch piece monoco fabric, 28 count

4mm silk embroidery ribbon (see color chart)

Scissors

Large-eyed embroidery needle

Needle

Thread

Embroidery hoop (optional)

2 pieces plain white cotton cloth, larger than embroidery hoop (optional)

1 When using an embroidery hoop, protect fabric by placing 2 pieces of thin white cloth between fabric and hoop. Cut a hole in middle of each piece of cloth large enough to expose pattern area. Place pieces on each side of fabric you will be embroidering, with holes over work area, and place all layers in embroidery hoop. Always take work out of hoop when you are not working on the project.

2 Transfer pattern to plain white paper, and tape to a sunny window. Trace pattern onto fabric using #2 pencil. Use 12-inch pieces of ribbon when embroidering. Embroider design in following order: roses with dusty rose; blue flowers using French blue and straight stitch; daisies using beauty and French knots; wisteria using iris and wild rose and French knots; stems using moss and stem stitch; leaves using moss and straight stitch. Flower centers are buttermilk French knots. (See finished photograph for color placement.) With needle and thread, sew loose ends of ribbon to other ribbon so ends do not show.

Note

See Craft Techniques for ribbon embroidery instructions on pages 8–9.

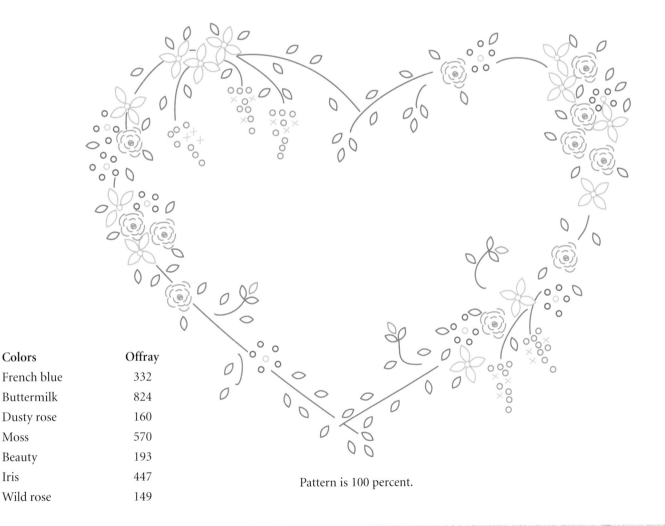

Pattern is 100 percent.

Colors	Offray
French blue	332
Buttermilk	824
Dusty rose	160
Moss	570
Beauty	193
Iris	447
Wild rose	149

Garden Fence Wreath

If fences make good neighbors, then this wreath will make a great gift for your favorite next-door friend!

What You'll Need

- 14-inch grapevine wreath
- 18-gauge wire
- Wire cutters
- 6-inch wooden gate
- White acrylic paint
- Paintbrush
- 3½-inch clay pot
- 46 inches floral print ribbon, 2½ inches wide
- Scissors
- Fabric glue
- Floral picks
- Florist tape
- 3 strands natural raffia, 36 inches each
- 3½ × 3½-inch block floral foam
- Cool-temp glue gun, glue sticks
- Wood straw
- 3-inch mushroom bird
- 2½-inch nest
- 3 stems green vinyl ivy, 18 inches each
- 12 stems assorted silk florals with leaves: white, pink, blue
- 4-inch birch wreath
- 1-inch egg

1 Cut a length of wire about 8 inches long. To make a hanger, twist wire around a few branches on back of wreath and make a loop.

2 Paint gate white. Let dry. Paint rim of clay pot white. Let dry.

3 From raffia, make a 3-loop bow with long tails. Secure bow with wire and attach to a floral pick; wrap pick with florist tape. Set aside. Cut 2 lengths of ribbon, one 10 inches and one 36 inches; angle cut ends of ribbon; seal ends with fabric glue. Make a 2-loop bow from 36-inch piece of ribbon. Secure with wire. Attach ribbon to a floral pick; wrap pick with florist tape. Place a wire in the center of the remaining piece of ribbon, and attach it to a floral pick. Wrap pick with florist tape. Set ribbons aside.

4 Wire gate to left side of wreath. Glue floral foam into pot. Cover top of foam with wood straw, and glue in place. Glue a floral pick into bottom of bird; glue bird in nest. Insert and glue nest into top right side of pot. Wire clay pot to right front of fence.

5 Glue a stem of ivy up left side of wreath. Cut remaining ivy into smaller pieces, and glue around lower right side, bottom, and left side of wreath.

6 Glue stems of flowers around ivy. Place larger flowers near bottom of wreath.

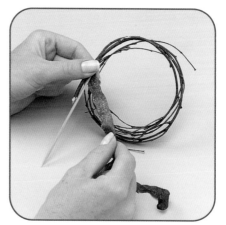

8 Gently separate 4-inch birch wreath. Attach birch pieces to picks; wrap picks with florist tape. Insert and glue birch pieces into wreath and pot.

7 Insert and glue 10-inch ribbon under fence, and glue tails along each side of wreath. Insert and glue 2-loop bow above pick of 10-inch ribbon. Glue remaining tails near bottom of wreath.

9 Insert and glue raffia bow into left side of pot. Glue egg inside pot.

Lemonade Pitcher and Glasses

Make that summer thirst-quenching treat even
more special. Lemonade never tasted so good!

What You'll Need

Clear glass pitcher and tall glasses

Pencil

White paper

Scissors

Sticky notes

Overhead projector pen

Cotton swabs

Acrylic enamel paints: cadmium yellow, lemon yellow, true blue

Palette

Paintbrushes: ¼-inch flat, liner

1 Wash and dry pitcher and glasses. Painting must be done on a clean, oil-free surface.

2 Trace lemon patterns (see the following page) onto white paper. Cut out. Trace patterns onto sticky notes at sticky edge, and cut out. For pitcher, lay lemon patterns on sticky edge of sticky notes and draw a line around them about ⅛ inch larger than patterns on all sides.

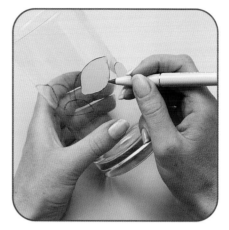

3 Stick lemon, lemon slice, and lemon wedge patterns onto glass surface about 2 inches from bottom (3 inches for pitcher). Draw around patterns with overhead projector pen. Move patterns around glass, and repeat. Continue until glass has been circled. If there are any stray pen marks on glass inside traced patterns, carefully remove with slightly damp cotton swab.

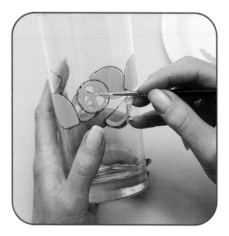

4 Squirt small amount of cadmium yellow paint onto palette. Using flat brush, fill in whole lemons with paint. Be careful not to touch traced outline with paintbrush. Use liner brush to paint along curved edge of lemon wedges. For lemon slices, paint outside circle then put

dot in center and paint 5 spokes radiating out to form lemon segments. Let dry 1 hour before applying second coat of paint.

5 Squirt a small puddle of lemon yellow paint onto palette. Fill in remaining portions of lemon wedges and slices. Let dry 1 hour, and apply second coat. If more coats of paint are necessary, be sure to let paint dry 1 hour between coats.

6 Carefully remove pen lines with slightly damp cotton swab.

7 Pour small amount of blue paint onto clean palette. Use flat brush to paint a checkerboard pattern about ½ inch from bottom of glass. (Use thick layer of glass at bottom as a guideline to keep checkerboard straight, or use overhead projector pen to draw line ½ inch from bottom of glass.) Let paint dry 1 hour between coats.

8 Let paint cure 24 hours. Follow paint manufacturer's instructions for a dishwasher-safe finish.

Patterns are 100 percent.

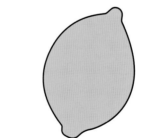

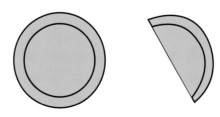

Mirrored Flowers Frame

*Mirror, mirror on the wall—this mirror is the fairest
of them all! Add silk pansies to a plain frame
for a beautiful addition to your foyer.*

What You'll Need

Picture frame

Green sheet moss

Hot glue gun, glue sticks

2 yards pansy ribbon

Scissors

9 silk pansies

Assorted small dried flower heads: larkspur, globe amaranth, American statice, ammobium

Assorted dried fillers: sweet Annie, plumosa, myrtle leaves

3 Glue a silk pansy to center of each bow. Add a pansy at the top and bottom of frame between bows.

4 On one side of frame, glue on a pansy. On other side, glue on 2 pansies.

1 Glue moss over front of frame; some moss can hang over sides.

5 Hot glue remaining assorted flowers and fillers on frame. For an extra touch, sprinkle frame with your favorite essential oil.

2 Cut ribbon into 4 equal pieces. Make 4 small bows, and hot glue a bow in each corner.

Posies a Plenty

A soft delicate collar of lace surrounds this basket.
The profusion of colors, shapes, and sizes
of flowers creates a touch of beauty.

What You'll Need

Round basket

3½ feet lace ribbon
(3 times circumference of basket)

Hot glue gun, glue sticks

Dry floral foam

Serrated knife

Green sheet moss

Craft pins

22-gauge stem wire

Wire cutters

3 silk blue hydrangeas

3 silk pink roses

7 silk pansies

3 silk purple dried-look asters with buds

3 silk pink dried-look asters with buds

4 silk stems cream statice

2 silk cream sweet William with buds

2 silk cream/burgundy sweet William
with buds

Floral picks (optional)

1 Using glue gun, glue ribbon around lip of basket, gathering ribbon as you go. Cut floral foam to fit basket, and place inside. Using craft pins, cover foam with sheet moss. Cut 2 pieces of wire twice the height of the floral foam plus 10 inches. Bend 1 wire into a large U shape, and push this up through basket and into foam at 1 side of foam block. With both ends of wire protruding from foam, twist wire ends together, and conceal ends in moss. Repeat with other wire on other side of foam block.

3 Place pansies and asters to create a rounded shape. Place a few flowers around the perimeter also. If stems of flowers are too short, add length by taping floral picks to stems.

4 Fill in design with statice and sweet William.

2 (Glue each flower before placing into foam.) To establish perimeter of design, place blue hydrangeas and pink roses around sides. Use wire cutters to cut flowers to desired lengths.

Vegetable Fruit Basket

*Use a combination of dried and silk fruits and vegetables
to create this stunning kitchen accessory.*

What You'll Need

12×6½-inch oval bark basket

Dry floral foam, 12×6½-inch piece

Craft knife

Cool-temp glue gun, glue sticks

Green garden moss

2 green vinyl ivy stems, 18 inches each

Floral picks

Florist tape: brown or green

Floral wire

Pencil

2 assorted color silk grape stems, 12 inches each

3 red vinyl apples, 2½ inches each

6 to 12 stems assorted vinyl fruits and vegetables with leaves (figs, squash, cut plums, etc.)

3-inch dried artichoke

2 to 4 stems dried red, orange, or yellow peppers, 1 to 3 inches each

6 to 12 stems dried yellow yarrow

2 to 4 stems dried blue or purple hydrangeas

4-inch birch wreath

12-inch straight birch bunch (2 to 4 stems secured with tape)

1 Cut floral foam to fit basket. Glue into place; cover foam with moss.

2 Separate ivy stems into 8 to 12 pieces. Attach each piece to a pick; secure with florist tape. Insert ivy around edge of basket.

3 To make wrapped wire squiggles, wrap thin wires tightly with florist tape. Wind wrapped wire around a pencil.

4 Remove wrapped wire, and attach to a floral pick. Secure with florist tape. Insert into arrangement.

5 Keep grapes in small bunches. Separate other fruits into individual pieces. Attach each piece to a pick, and secure with florist tape.

Insert into basket in a pleasing manner. Let some fruit hang over sides.

6 Insert figs and artichoke. Divide peppers into smaller bunches. Attach each bunch to a pick, and secure with florist tape; insert peppers into arrangement. Let some peppers hang over sides.

7 Separate yarrow and hydrangeas into small bunches. Attach each to a pick and secure with florist tape. Fill in remaining spaces in arrangement.

8 Gently separate birch wreath. Attach birch pieces to picks, and secure with florist tape. Insert birch into arrangement; let some loop over sides. Insert straight birch sticks near center.

Veggie Floor Mat

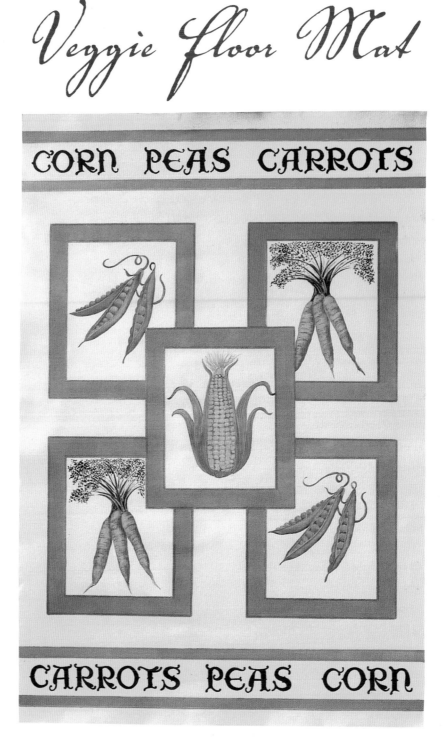

This mat will entice people out to your garden; it would also look great as a wall hanging in your family room or sunporch!

What You'll Need

Canvas floor mat, 24×35 inches

Acrylic paint: buttermilk, hauser light green, pumpkin, leaf green, olive green, cadmium orange, cadmium yellow

Paintbrushes: 2-inch flat, #1 liner, #4 shader, #3 round, #8 shader

Yardstick

Medium and hard pencils

Triangle

Eraser

1-inch masking tape

Small, flat sponge

Permanent gold marker

Tracing paper

Transfer paper

Polyurethane varnish

Paint thinner

Note

See Craft Techniques for decorative painting instructions on pages 9–11.

1 Using 2-inch brush, paint canvas buttermilk. Let dry overnight.

2 For borders, use medium pencil and measure from top and bottom edges. Lightly draw lines at 1 inch, 1½ inches, 2 inches, 3¼ inches, 3¾ inches, and 4¼ inches. You will paint borders between the 1 and 1½ inch lines and between the 3¾ and 4¼ inch lines. The other 2 lines are for placing patterns (see step 5).

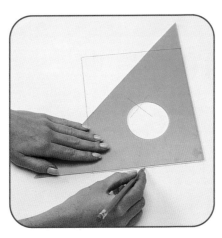

3 To find placement of center rectangle, lay yardstick diagonally across mat from edge of last top ruled line on right side to last bottom ruled line on left side. Draw a 2-inch line at center. Repeat in opposite direction and draw another line, forming an X. Center of X is center of the corn rectangle. Measure 3¼ inches from right and left sides of center and 4 inches from top and bottom of center. Draw a rectangle, using the triangle. Measure 1 inch around all sides of center rectangle, and draw a border. Position remaining 6½×8-inch rectangles 3 inches from border and 2¾ inches from sides. (See finished photo for placement.) Draw 1-inch borders outside all rectangles. Erase unnecessary lines.

4 Tape around inside and outside edges of rectangles and around ½-inch border strips (at top and bottom of mat). Burnish tape with fingernail. Sponge hauser light green stripes on top and bottom, and sponge rectangles with pumpkin. Let dry. Remove tape. Outline all lines with gold marker. Let dry.

5 Trace patterns (on pages 127–129) onto tracing paper, including lines on lettering. Tape words in place, aligning lines on paper with those on canvas. With hard pencil, transfer words only. Transfer vegetables to rectangles, centering designs.

6 Fill in lettering with leaf green, using #1 and #4 brushes. Let dry. Erase pencil lines.

7 With #3 round brush, basecoat carrot tops, corn husks, areas around peas, pea stems, and outside of pods with leaf green. Basecoat pod edge lines olive green, carrots cadmium orange, and corn cadmium yellow. Dry brush corn silk olive green. Leave tiny lines of buttermilk between objects of the same color that join (such as husk of corn).

8 Using hauser light green, dry brush over pea pods, leaving bottoms darker. Shade vines and top of middle pod, add additional dots and lines to carrot tops, and make thin vertical lines on corn husks.

9 Use olive green to add more shading to pea pods at tops and vines and to carrot stems.

10 Create shading on bottom of peas with leaf green, and add highlights on tops of peas with olive green; blend colors in centers of peas. Soften pod center lines with a wash of leaf green.

11 Mix leaf green and pumpkin to make khaki brown, and outline corn kernels. Wash khaki over kernels on both sides, leaving center of cob clear. Highlight center kernel tops with buttermilk, blend mix of buttermilk and cadmium yellow into kernel centers, and wash khaki onto bottoms. Dot a few areas between kernels with hauser light green and pumpkin. Use khaki and buttermilk to shape top of corn and enhance corn silk lines. Wash over husk with hauser light green, making sure lines remain. Wash bottom section with leaf green.

12 With #4 brush, dry brush pumpkin over carrots, starting at left edge and working to right, leaving some cadmium orange showing. Highlight center of carrots with mix of pumpkin and buttermilk. Define ridges and make a few hairs at root ends with cadmium orange with #1 brush. Let dry overnight.

13 Varnish following manufacturer's directions.

Enlarge pattern 125 percent.

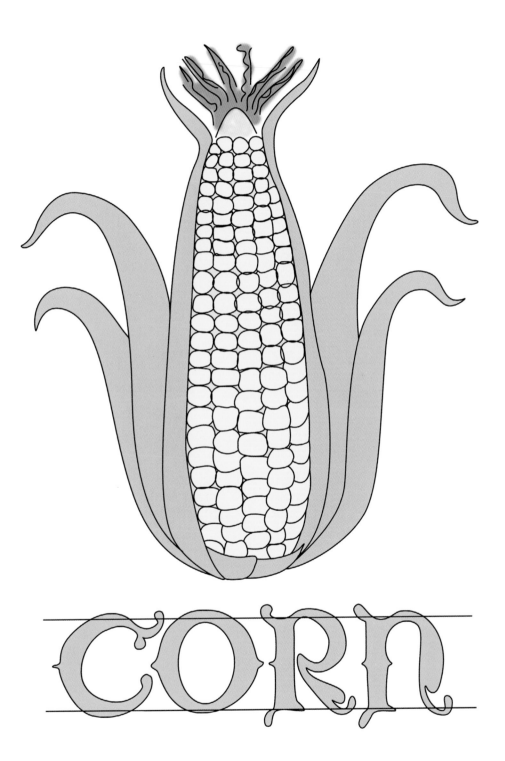

Enlarge pattern 125 percent.

Enlarge pattern 125 percent.

Summer Wedding Basket

This charming Victorian basket has a subtle combination of fragrant fresh and dried blooms of heather, statice, rose, caspia, and hydrangea.

What You'll Need

❧

6×4×9-inch cream basket

11 to 12 stems dried yellow roses

11 stems fresh or dried purple statice

11 stems fresh or dried caspia

11 stems fresh or dried pink heather

3 to 4 stems fresh or dried lemon leaf (salal)

12 to 14 stems dried pink larkspur

12 stems dried green lepidium

12 stems dried green broom

1 package dried white campo flowers

7 to 10 stems dried hydrangeas

Wire cutters

22-gauge floral wire

Hot glue gun, glue sticks

Sheet moss

2 Slip wire ends of flower bundles through open slats of basket rim, and twist wire ends inside basket. Overlap each flower bundle onto basket rim as you wire. Secure bundles with hot glue if necessary.

3 Clip excess wire ends. Hot glue moss over exposed wire inside basket.

1 Cut all dried and fresh flowers from 7 to 10 inches long. Wire mixture of flowers into 11 to 12 bundles.

Tip

❧

Color intensity, quality, and selection is more readily available when using fresh flowers and foliage appropriate for drying. By allowing the fresh flowers to dry naturally in a week or less, your results will be a beautiful permanent display.

Birch Bark Candlesticks

*The rustic splendor of these candlesticks will look
lovely in any decor. And, what is even better,
anyone can make them for their home!*

What You'll Need

White birch logs, approximately 3 inches in diameter

Safety goggles, work gloves

Crosscut handsaw

Ruler

Sandpaper

Marking pen

⅜-inch variable-speed drill with a ¾-inch bit

Note

Never leave burning candles unattended.

2 Stand cut logs upright to make certain they stand straight. Use sandpaper if necessary to smooth top and bottom ends.

1 Always use safety glasses or goggles when working with wood to shield your face and eyes from flying wood chips and sawdust. Using handsaw, cut three 3-inch-diameter branches into 3 sizes, ranging from 2½ to 8 inches high.

3 Mark center of log with ruler and pen.

4 Using drill and ¾-inch bit, drill a hole for candle on center mark, approximately 1 inch deep.

Gazebo Birdhouse

*Start your spring with this welcoming gazebo birdhouse.
The roof is removable for easy cleaning—generations
of birds can visit you year after year!*

What You'll Need

Wood gazebo birdhouse

Sandpaper

Tack cloth

Acrylic paint: snow white, settlers blue, grey sky, thicket

Paintbrushes: ½-inch flat, #2 flat, 10/0 liner, ⅜-inch angle

Water-base wood sealer or varnish

Tracing paper

Pencil

Transfer paper or carbon paper

Matte spray finish

Note

See Craft Techniques for decorative painting instructions on pages 9–11.

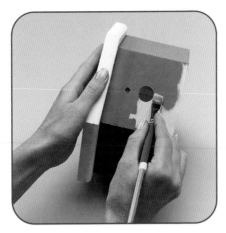

1 Prepare birdhouse by sanding and using a tack cloth to remove dust. For basecoating only, mix equal parts of paint and water-base wood sealer. Basecoat following: base, underneath base, roof, eaves, perch, and ball decor on rooftop with snow white; outside walls with settlers blue. No other mixing with varnish is necessary. Do not paint inside opening or inside birdhouse; birds will not visit. Let dry. Trace patterns on page 136. Apply each panel of roof and walls by repeating patterns on roof and sides.

2 Base railing and trim work with snow white. Let dry. This may take 2 or more coats of paint for total coverage. Apply detail pattern to

railings. Line all board separation or connections and roof shingles with grey sky. Let dry. Float all connections on railings and underneath each row of shingles with grey sky.

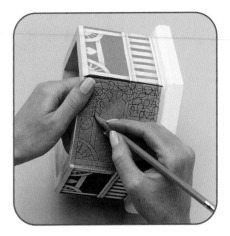

3 Apply detail pattern for ivy. Base leaves with thicket. Replace ball decor.

4 Spray with matte spray finish. Glue roof to body for an indoor birdhouse, or attach a small craft hinge for outdoor use.

Brown Paper Plant Wraps

For unusual hostess gifts, make these stunning plant wraps.
They'd also make a great centerpiece for your next party.

What You'll Need

Brown paper

Ruler

Pencil

Scissors

Plastic storage bags

Pins

Thread: green, orange, red, peacock blue, yellow, white

Sewing machine

Pinking shears

Glue stick

Red felt-tip marker

½ to 1 yard for each wrap: jute, dyed jute, raffia, ribbon, or fancy cord

Machine Sewing on Paper

Sewing machines are designed to sew on fabric—not paper. Some irregularities are to be expected in your finished product. Accept that a small number of skipped stitches will happen. If it happens a lot, replace the needle. A needle that is dull or has a burr on the tip can cause skipped stitches. Also, sewing on paper can fray thread—rethread your machine at the first sign of fray.

A needle makes a permanent hole in paper. Learn to stop and start with precision. It is helpful to let up on the pedal, and hand crank the last few stitches to a critical stopping point.

Paper can tear easily. If your machine jams, don't tug. Cut away all threads to avoid leaving a hole in your work.

Do not set your stitch length too close when making a satin stitch on paper: Needle holes too close together will make a perforated line and tear. (Repairs and/or reinforcements can be made on the back side of your work using tape or a paper patch.)

To end, pull all threads to back of paper. Glue first, then snip ends short. Any threads left on front can also be glued and snipped. Never backstitch on paper!

Don't worry too much about what will happen to a fancy stitch when you turn a corner. Just sew on the line and try to pivot when the needle is on the right side.

When you pivot on a corner, make the turn with the needle in the paper. The needle should be on its way up.

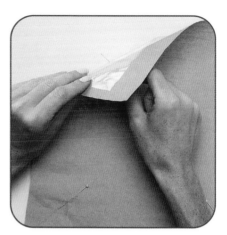

1 Cut an 11-inch square of brown paper for each plant wrap. Pin a plastic bag to each piece of paper. Starting at outside edge, measure and draw guidelines ½ inch apart moving to center. Make 4 lines on green and orange wraps, and make 3 lines on red and blue wraps.

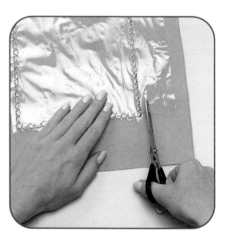

2 For all wrap colors, stitch innermost line first, securing plastic. Turn paper over, and cut off excess plastic. Though not completely waterproof, this plastic liner will prevent a damp flowerpot from spoiling your wrap.

3 Green wrap: Trim outside edge with pinking shears. On fourth and third lines, sew a straight stitch. Sew a curved line between 2 straight rows. Use wide satin stitch setting to sew satin stitch on first 2 guidelines. Pull thread ends through to back; glue and trim.

4 Red wrap: Trim outside edge with pinking shears. On innermost row, sew a pointed decorative stitch. On second row, sew a wide zigzag stitch. Sew a straight stitch between these rows. On first row, sew a curved stitch. Between first and second rows, sew a wide satin stitch. Sew a straight stitch between curved stitch and outside edge. Use red marker to color from curved stitch to outside edge. Pull thread ends through to back; glue and trim.

5 Orange wrap: On 3 inner rows, sew wavy lines. On first row, sew a wide satin stitch. Between first row and edge, sew a wide satin stitch using yellow thread. Pull threads through to back; glue and trim.

6 Blue wrap: On third and first rows, sew a wavy stitch. On second row, working from edge to edge, sew a wide satin stitch using white thread. As close to the cut edge as you can, stitch a wide blue satin stitch. Pull thread ends through to back; glue and trim.

7 Fold wrap around flowerpot, and secure with jute or other ribbon, as desired.

Garden Lanterns

*Create a fairyland to enchant your party-going guests!
These delightful lanterns are fun and can
become a family project.*

What You'll Need

Cardboard

#2 pencil

Scissors

Cream parchment paper

Pinking shears

SumiBrush pen (available at art stores)

Soft eraser

Art markers: grass green, true green, Spanish orange, hot pink, process red, limepeel green, chartreuse

Craft glue

Strand white mini-lights

Small vinyl-covered paper clips

2 Cut out all shades, using pinking shears for 2 short sides and long side without circular opening. Use plain scissors to cut remaining long side, carefully cutting out circle. Cut about 7 short (about ¹⁄₁₆ inch) notches around circle.

4 Before using the SumiBrush pen, practice making thick and thin lines. Try to keep lines loose and relaxed. Outline all designs on shades. Gently erase any carbon or pencil marks.

1 Trace pattern onto cardboard, and cut out. Trace around template (see page 143) to make the number of shades you'd like to create. Three patterns will fit on an 8½×11-inch sheet of parchment.

3 Transfer a design (see page 143) to each side of a shade. (You can use transfer paper, or use #2 pencil and lightly color across design on wrong side. Then place design on paper faceup, and trace pattern onto shade.) Pull shade into final round shape, and check to see that design is positioned well. Make any adjustments, and proceed to transfer remaining designs.

5 Begin using thick end of art markers to fill in designs. Again, be loose. Don't follow outlines too closely. Allow color to go outside lines or well within them, sometimes allowing parchment to show through. Color each as follows: make leaves grass green and true green; color flowers Spanish orange, hot pink, process red, and limepeel green; color butterflies Spanish orange, process red, chartreuse, and true green; color watering cans process red, Spanish orange, chartreuse, hot pink, and limepeel green.

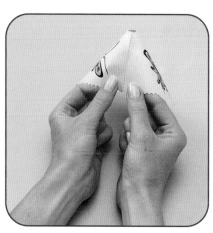

6 Apply narrow strip of glue to side B only. Do one shade at a time as glue dries quickly. Carefully bend shade into curve. Position side A over side B about ¼ inch. When sides are positioned, press together and smooth seam. Repeat for all shades.

8 Gently pull open paper clip so it is spread into a V. Thread clip onto cord.

9 Settle bulb and clip back into neck of shade, which should be loose but not able to fall off. If necessary, a stitch can be made with a needle and embroidery floss to tighten shade opening around base of light. Attach remainder of shades in same manner. Handle shades carefully to prevent dents and creases.

7 Turn shade upside-down. Take a strand of mini-lights and, just beneath a light, pinch cord together. Carefully push light through hole until enough cord is exposed on inside of shade so you will be able to thread a paper clip through a strand of cord. Take care not to damage opening of shade.

Patterns are 100 percent.

Picket Fence Shelf

*Now you can have your own white picket fence—
even if you live in an apartment. This shelf is the perfect
place to display your prize posies!*

What You'll Need

❧

2 sections redwood border fencing, 36 inches long

Safety goggles, work gloves

Crosscut handsaw

¾-inch pine board, 6×32 inches

⅜-inch variable-speed drill and bit (for Phillips-head screws) or Phillips-head screwdriver

2½-inch Phillips-head drywall screws

Heavy-duty staple gun, staples

Marking pencil

Ruler

Carpenter's wood filler, spatula

White latex satin (or semi-gloss) enamel paint

Paintbrush

Sandpaper (optional)

1 Place 1 section of border fencing on a clean, level surface. Using crosscut handsaw, cut long pickets (that were intended to be inserted in ground) even with shorter pickets. This is front shelf border.

2 Using electric drill or screwdriver and 2½-inch drywall screws, attach front shelf border, pickets pointing up, to ¾-inch pine board along lower rail.

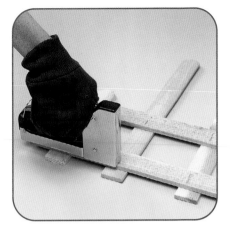

3 For back shelf border: Carefully remove 2 tall ground-stake pickets from second section of fencing. Saw pointed bottom edges so they are straight. Reposition tall pickets, making sure bottom edges are even with other pickets. Use staples to attach tall pickets to fence brace from back.

4 Using ruler, mark a point 3 inches down from 2 tall pickets. Drill a counter-sunk hole at this location. These holes are to be used to attach shelf to wall.

5 Lay attached fencing facedown on work surface. Attach back section to shelf in same manner as you attached front (see step 2).

6 Fill in front drywall screws with wood filler according to package directions. Allow to dry, and sand lightly if necessary.

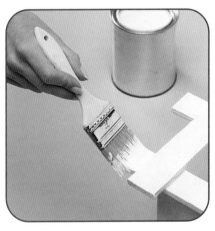

7 Paint shelf white. Let dry overnight. Using drywall screws, attach shelf to wall.

Tip
❧

Leave the shelf unpainted for a more rustic look, or personalize it to match the color theme of your garden.

Charming Picture Frame

*Add romance and elegance to a plain brass frame
by gluing on a few charms. Create the perfect
place for a very special photo!*

What You'll Need

Brass charms: locket, frame and frame back, assorted birds, flowers, hat, etc. (enough to cover frame)

Rubbing alcohol

Waxed paper

Glossy spray varnish

4×6-inch brass picture frame

Flower pictures to fit charm frame and locket

Scissors

Glue stick

Pliers

4 corner brass filigrees and filigrees to fill in remaining space on frame

Disposable plate

Industrial strength adhesive

Toothpicks

1 Work in a well-ventilated area while making this project. Clean charms with rubbing alcohol. Lay charms on waxed paper, and spray with varnish. Let dry.

2 Cut picture to fit charm frame. Using glue stick, adhere picture to frame back. Use pliers to bend prongs over frame back, securing picture in frame. Cut photograph to fit locket. Insert.

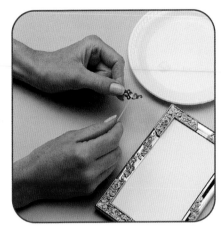

3 Arrange filigrees on frame. Squeeze adhesive onto plate, and use toothpick to apply glue to backs of filigrees and onto areas of the frame where they will be placed. Adhere filigrees to frame.

4 Arrange charms, locket, and charm frame on top of filigrees. Adhere one charm at a time by applying adhesive to back of charm and to desired area of frame. Set charm in place. Repeat until all charms are glued on. Let frame lay flat for 24 hours.

Birds of a Feather

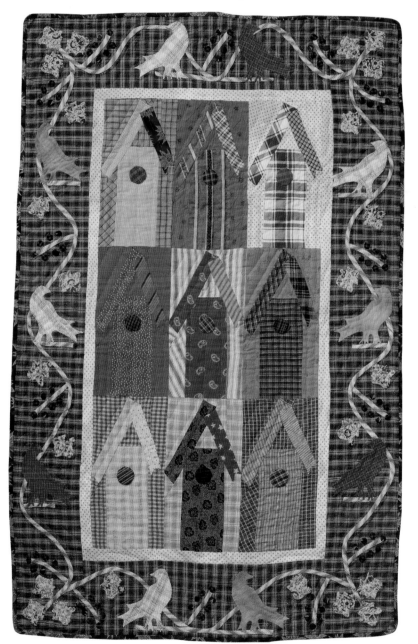

Create a family heirloom—generations will enjoy this quilted work of art.

What You'll Need

Template plastic

Pencil

Ruler

Utility scissors

Material: 1/8 yard or scraps of 18 different lights, mediums, and darks for birdhouses and background blocks

9 scraps at least 2-inch square for birdhouse holes using variations of the same color tones

9 scraps at least 8×2½ inches for appliquéd roofs using variations of the same color tones

1/8 yard tan print for inner border

3/4 yard blue plaid for outer border

1/8 yard tan/blue/red print for leaves

1/8 yard dark red solid or print for berries

1/8 yard each gold, red, and tan/blue plaid for birds

3/4 yard tan/blue stripe for vine

1/3 yard dark red solid or print for binding

1½ yards backing material

Fabric scissors

Sewing machine

Thread: neutral color for piecing blocks and colors to match appliqué pieces

Paper

Tweezers

Iron, ironing board

1 package low-loft batting, 45×60 inches

Notes

Quilt Dimensions: 32×50 inches

Add ¼ inch to pattern pieces for seam allowances. Unless otherwise indi-cated, the pattern lines are sewing lines, not cutting lines.

See Craft Techniques for general quilting instructions on pages 13–17.

1 To make birdhouse block tem-plates (pattern pieces A through H on page 151): Place template plastic over pattern, and trace pat-tern piece outlines. Using a ruler, mark ¼-inch seam allowance around outer edge of pattern pieces on plastic. Cut out along inner edge of outside line.

2 To make appliqué templates (pattern pieces I, J, bird, leaf, and berry on page 151): Make the appliqué templates the size that you want the figures to appear on quilt. The seam allowances are added on the material. Cut out along inner edge of outside line.

3 For each birdhouse block: cut pieces A, B, E, G, and H from same material. Cut pieces C and F from same material. Cut pieces H and J from different materials. (For each block, there will be 4 dif-ferent materials used.) Using tem-plates, mark pieces A, B, D, E, G, and H onto right side of background material using a sharp pencil. Using fabric scissors, cut out pieces. Using templates, mark pieces C and F on right side of birdhouse material. Using fabric scissors, cut out pieces.

4 Piece block in the following sequence (following pattern layout): Sew pieces B and D to C. Sew A to top of piece BDC. Sew pieces E and G to piece F. Sew piece ABCD to piece EFG. Sew piece H to side to complete block. Make 9 blocks.

5 To mark birdhouse appliqué pieces (I and J), place template on right side of fabric. Draw around template using a sharp pencil. Cut out piece J (birdhouse hole) from 2-inch squares, adding ¼-inch seam allowance. To make a circle, cut out paper the size of the circle template (don't add seam allowance). Sew a running stitch slightly in from edge of fabric starting with a knotted end. Lay paper piece in center of material, and pull loose end of thread around paper—snug but not too tight. Secure with a backstitch. Appliqué piece in place with thread that matches appliqué; turn work over and snip fabric behind circle. Pull out paper with tweezers.

6 Mark and cut piece I. Press seam allowance under, and appliqué in place.

7 Sew birdhouse blocks into 3 rows with 3 houses in each row. Sew rows together to make quilt top.

8 For borders: From tan, cut two 1½×36-inch strips and two 1½×20-inch strips. Sew 36-inch strips to sides of quilt top. Sew 20-inch strips to top and bottom of quilt top. From blue plaid, cut two 6½×20-inch strips and two 6½×50-inch strips. Sew 20-inch strips to top and bottom of quilt. Sew 50-inch strips to sides of quilt.

9 To make bias binding: Cut a 21-inch square from tan and blue stripe material. Cut square in half diagonally, making 2 triangles. With right sides facing, sew triangles together (see illustrations below). Mark cutting lines 1 inch apart parallel to long bias edges. Cut into strips. To join strips, lay them perpendicular to each other with right sides facing. Stitch across strips, making a diagonal seam. Using hot steam iron, press under ¼ inch on each side of binding, leaving a ½-inch finished bias binding strip that is approximately 362 inches long.

10 From bias length, cut six 3½-inch bird perches for sides, two 10½-inch bird perches for top and bottom, and fourteen 4-inch berry stems.

11 Using finished photo as a guide, sew bias strips to outer border of quilt.

12 Using appliqué templates, mark 2 birds and 1 reverse bird (turn template over before marking) on right side of red material. Adding ¼-inch seam allowance, cut out. Mark and cut 1 bird and 3 reverse birds from tan/blue plaid, 2 birds and 1 reverse bird from gold material, 24 leaves from tan/blue/red print, and 95 berries from dark red solid or print.

13 Press seam allowances under and, using finished photo as a guide, place and sew birds, leaves, and berries to quilt.

14 Cut batting and backing fabric larger than quilt top. Lay backing fabric facedown, lay batting on top, and quilt top faceup. Baste layers together. Hand or machine quilt layers together. Trim batting and backing.

15 Cut binding fabric into 1½-inch strips (seam allowances are included), and join strips to create one very long strip that is at least 168 inches long. Sew binding fabric to quilt top, and turn binding to back of quilt and hand-stitch in place.

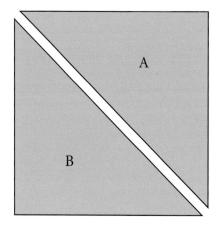

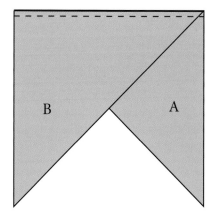

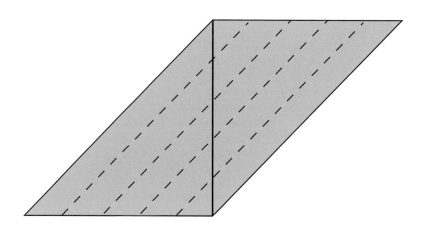

Enlarge patterns 150 percent.

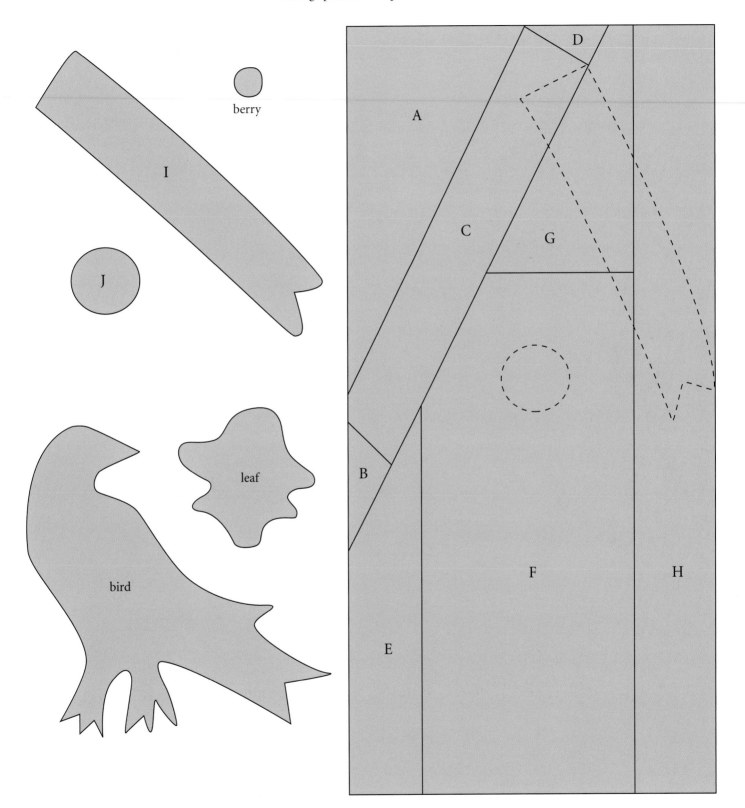

berry

I

J

leaf

bird

A

C

D

B

G

E

F

H

Brick Doorstop

Welcome everyone into your room with this adorable doorstop made from a simple brick. The flower shop look is sure to be a hit!

What You'll Need
🌿

Brick

Acrylic paint: buttermilk, red iron oxide, teal green, sable brown, ebony black, thicket, lemon yellow, pumpkin

Paintbrushes: ½-inch flat, #2 flat, ⅜-inch angle, 10/0 liner

Tracing paper

Transfer paper

Pencil

Matte finishing spray

Note
🌿

See Craft Techniques for decorative painting instructions on pages 9–11.

1 Wash brick with water. Let dry. Basecoat entire brick with buttermilk. Let dry. (If brick has a lot of texture, the drying time will increase.)

2 Apply color change pattern (see page 154). Base roof, flowerpot, and flower boxes with red iron oxide. Base door, shutters, and window frames with teal green. Base tree trunk with sable brown. Let dry.

3 Apply detail pattern (shingles, shutter lines, door dimension, flowerpot, bricks, and leaf placement). Float and line shingles, shutters, tree trunk, door, flower boxes, and flowerpot with ebony black. Make doorknob with ebony black using wooden end of paintbrush. Wash rooftop with water-diluted ebony black.

4 Using a wash of red iron oxide, apply faded bricks. Let dry. Using thicket and #2 flat, apply leaves to flower boxes and tree.

5 Dot flowers on tree and in flower boxes with lemon yellow and pumpkin using end of the brush.

6 Line "WELCOME" with ebony black. Let dry. Finish with complete spray of matte finishing spray.

Tip
🌿

Paint a village of brick houses for a border edging a small garden plot. The spray finish will protect your houses from the elements.

Where Love Birds Meet

Invite all types of birds into your yard with this great feeder.
This functional bird feeder will be the envy of your neighbors.

What You'll Need
🌿

Wood bird feeder

Acrylic paint: country red, sky grey, snow white, neutral grey, sweetheart pink, mink tan, blue heaven, harvest gold, raspberry sherbet, dark chocolate, denim blue, ebony black

Wood sealer

Paintbrushes: ½-inch flat, #2 flat, ⅜-inch angle, 10/0 liner

Eraser

½-inch cellophane tape

Matte finishing spray

Notes
🌿

See Craft Techniques for decorative painting instructions on pages 9–11.

When basecoating in step 1, add 1 part wood sealer to 3 parts paint. This adds your first coat of color along with sealing wood.

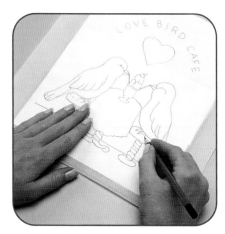

1 Basecoat roof and eaves with country red; side walls (inside and out), sides, and underneath bottom tray with sky grey; and top inside of tray with snow white. Let dry. Apply side pattern (see page 158) on both sides.

2 Base birds, tablecloth, sundae glass, straws, and ice cream with snow white. This base will yield brighter colors. Let dry. Base stool and table legs with neutral grey. Apply detail pattern for the bird, sundae, and tablecloth plaid.

3 Base cherry, heart, and stool seats with country red. Base top scoop of ice cream with sweetheart pink and second scoop with mink tan. Base bird back, tail, wing, and top of head with blue heaven. Base beak and feet with harvest gold.

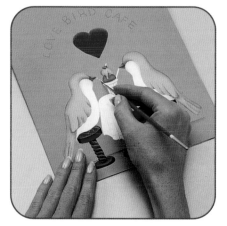

4 Float the white/blue separation area of bird with blue heaven so colors blend. Float top of heart, top of bird cheeks, and front edge of stool seat with sweetheart pink. Float pink ice cream with raspberry sherbet. Float chocolate ice cream with dark chocolate. Float sundae glass with sky grey. Float denim blue on birds' tails, wings, behind cheeks, across tops of heads, and on backs. Float a shade on stool seats, bottom of each twist on table and stool legs, floor line, and stem area of cherry with diluted ebony black. Float a highlight on the twists with sky grey. Float beak and feet with dark chocolate. Line straw stripes with country red.

(This should be placed at right angles to the first stripes.) Base stripes with diluted country red, and let dry. Remove tape.

5 Erase tablecloth pattern lines enough so they are just visible. Dilute country red, and apply one direction of tablecloth lines. Let dry. Apply lines in opposite direction using diluted country red. This will create the plaid effect. If necessary, apply another coat of red on small overlapping squares to deepen color. Let dry. Float shade on tablecloth with diluted ebony black.

7 Line entire pattern including "LOVE BIRD CAFE" with ebony black. Keep paint the consistency of ink for smoother, thinner lines.

6 For feed tray: Securely apply ½-inch stripes of tape spaced equally across one direction. (Make sure tape edges are secure to prevent bleeding under tape. Should bleeding occur, touch up with snow white when paint is dry.) Using diluted country red, base stripes and let dry completely. Remove tape, and apply new tape in opposite direction.

8 Apply roof pattern (pattern is repeated). Line entirely with ebony black, and let dry. Float a shade under each shingle with ebony black. Let dry. Spray feeder with matte finishing spray to seal.

Pattern is 100 percent.

Summer Garden Potpourri

"What is that wonderful smell?"
Potpourri brings the garden scent of summer's
bouquet into your home.

What You'll Need

🌿

⅛ cup orris (Fx)

⅓ cup vetiver (Fx)

½ cup oak moss (Fx)

1 teaspoon whole cloves (S)

½ teaspoon ground cinnamon (S)

3 drops lime oil

3 drops orange oil

9 drops Summer Garden oil

1 cup each dried yellow and
pink rose petals

1 cup Uva Ursi leaves

½ cup bay leaves

¼ cup dried orange peel

⅓ cup purple larkspur

1 tablespoon lavender seeds

Large nonporous bowl

Airtight container or plastic storage bag

3 to 4 whole dried assorted roses

3 to 4 pressed assorted flowers

Fx = Fixative   S = Spice

1 Mix all fixatives and spices in bowl. Add oils. Rub mixture with fingers to fix.

2 Add all ingredients up to and including lavender seeds to bowl. Mix thoroughly.

3 Place mixture in an airtight container, and leave it for 4 to 6 weeks in a dark place to cure. Stir mixture every few days to blend and distribute ingredients.

4 Transfer potpourri to a decorative container, and add whole dried roses and pressed flowers to decorate.

Tips

🌿

You can use food storage plastic seal bags for curing your potpourri. When fragrance has diminished, you can revitalize it by placing the potpourri back into a storage bag. Add a few drops of essential oils to some cotton balls, place them inside the bag, and seal it up. Leave cotton balls in bag for 2 to 3 days and then remove. Fragrance will be restored.

Potpourri Terminology

🌿

Potpourri is a fragrant mix of flowers, herbs, spices, leaves, seeds, fixatives, and essential oils that, when blended, create distinct fragrances.

There are five basic groups of ingredients in potpourri: flowers, spices, herbs, fixatives, and essential oils.

FLOWERS are the most important group because of the scents and the decorative additions. Flowers, flower petals and buds, wood, bark, or fruit peels are used extensively in potpourri blends. These materials will set the theme of your potpourri.

SPICES give potpourri its warmth and sweet smell. They add richness and character to the entire blend of the bouquet. Important spices commonly used are cinnamon, whole cloves, and nutmeg.

HERBS add a subtle background fragrance. Lavender is the most important and most frequently used herb in potpourri blends. Others, such as rosemary, lemon mint, bay leaf, and bergamot, are also widely used. These earthy fragrances add interest to the mix, giving it a complex quality.

FIXATIVES hold or fix and absorb the scents of all the other ingredients; often they contribute their own fragrance as well. The most commonly used are orris root (powder or pieces), gum benzoin, chopped corncob, and oak moss.

ESSENTIAL OILS can dictate the aroma or perfume of a potpourri entirely or can contribute to it, depending on how much you add to the mixture of botanicals. It is better to blend your oil combinations on a piece of thick paper first to develop new fragrances. Don't make mistakes on your plant materials.

Ribbon Trellis Frame

Bring an ivy trellis into your home and, unlike your outdoor ivy, it will last all year long.

What You'll Need

2 to 3 sprigs silk ivy

Scissors

Two 8×10-inch mats with 5×7-inch opening

Pencil

Ruler

Straightedge

Craft knife

Black permanent felt-tip marker

8×10-inch ready-made velvet frameback with stand

12×14-inch piece low-loft batting

Craft glue

Craft stick

12×14-inch piece natural evenweave linen

Iron

Masking tape

Tracing paper

Transfer paper

Tracing wheel

5 yards ecru ribbon, ¼ inch wide

Straight pins with ball tips

Embroidery needle

Ecru embroidery floss

Washable fabric marker

Heavy book

1 yard hook-and-loop tape

1 Most silk ivy is made up of 2-leaf sections with a stem. Cut stem, and pull off ivy sections. You will only use the small and medium leaves.

2 Take one mat and enlarge 5×7-inch opening: (Measure ¼ inch in from the inside opening and mark a line all around with a pencil.) Lay a straightedge on the line and cut away excess with a sharp craft knife. Blacken the outside edge (this mat only) with a felt-tip marker. Align this mat with frameback (wrong side), and trace a pencil line onto frameback around mat's inside opening. Put both pieces aside.

3 Glue batting on second mat. (Rub a thin coating of glue on mat; press batting on glue. Let dry briefly.) Trim batting even with mat edges. Put aside.

4 Press wrinkles out of linen. Tape linen on tabletop or cardboard using masking tape. Tape along edges, keeping fabric taut and straight. Transfer design (on page 166, enlarge to fit frame) to linen using tracing wheel. Leave work taped down until step 7.

5 Carefully pin ribbon along diagonal guidelines in one direction. Allow ribbon to extend about 1½ inches beyond borders of mat at inside and outside edges.

6 Next, pin ribbon in other diagonal direction, weaving over and under intersecting ribbons. You will have to adjust pins to allow ribbon to weave. Pin at each intersection. Untape work and remove from work surface.

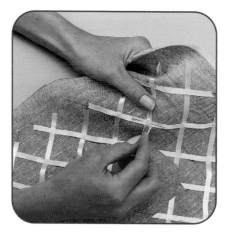

7 Thread needle with an 18-inch length of floss (3-ply), and embroider an X at every intersection to hold ribbon in place. Remove pins as you go. Secure each X at back with tiny stitches. (This X stitch is the standard cross-stitch.)

8 Lightly glue down any loose ribbon ends along inside and outside edges. Let dry 10 minutes. Trim to within 1 inch from edge of pattern. (Do not trim inside mat opening yet.) Transfer the 4 outer corner positions by putting a straight pin through to the wrong side, and marking each corner on the wrong side with a fabric marker. Remove straight pins.

9 Spread a thin layer of glue on batting already placed on mat. Place linen facedown on a clean work surface, and center mat on linen, batting side down, aligning at corners. Cut an X in the center, stopping ¼ inch from corners. Cut away all but 1 inch from linen.

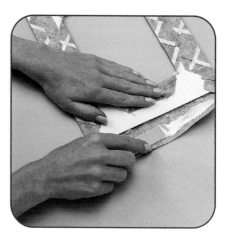

10 To stretch linen over mat: Fold corners over first, and glue in place. Next, fold and glue sides, keeping as flat as possible. Trim excess fabric where needed. Let dry.

11 On mat with black edging, spread glue over one side. Align this mat with the linen-covered mat, and glue together. Press under a heavy book, and allow to dry for 1 to 2 hours.

12 Cut eight 1-inch pieces from hook side of hook-and-loop tape, and stick 1 on each side of each corner of black-edged mat.

14 Position ivy sprigs randomly under ribbon on front of linen. When arrangement is pleasing, use straight pins to pin ivy in place. Hide pins under ribbon. Unruly ivy can be glued lightly in place.

Tip

Make smaller frames to give as gifts with the kids' school pictures—the grandparents will really appreciate the thoughtfulness. And, if Grandma's favorite flower is the rose, add those instead of the ivy. Make each frame a personal message of love!

13 Cut loop side of hook-and-loop tape to fit around pencil line on back of frameback. Photo or mirror can be placed in center and is held in place by hook-and-loop tape edge and mat edge.

Enlarge pattern 125 percent.

Beaded Birdhouse Treasures

This stunning tree full of birds and birdhouses is a must for the bird-lover in your midst. The beads add polish to the easy-to-do plastic canvas.

What You'll Need

14-count cream plastic canvas

Cream thread

Seed beads (see color key), 1 package each color

Ceramic birdhouse and bird buttons

Wooden window tree

Scissors

Small green garland

Hot glue gun, glue sticks

4 feet cream ribbon, ⅛ inch wide

Black embroidery floss

Note

See Craft Techniques for plastic canvas instructions on pages 6–8.

Color	Mill Hill #
Light green	525
Dark green	332
Brown	2023
Gold	0557
Pearl	479
Grey	150
Light yellow	2002
Dark yellow	128
Light blue	2007
Dark blue	020
Pink	62035
Red	165
White	3015
Black	2014

When all designs are finished, use a pair of sharp scissors and cut 1 row away from stitches to cut out design.

Wrap garland around limbs of tree, and attach each end with a drop of hot glue.

Cut ribbon into twelve 4-inch pieces. Stitch an ornament to center of a ribbon; tie ribbon around limb with a bow. Use a drop of hot glue on each bow to anchor it. Hot glue bird button to top of tree and birdhouse button to base.

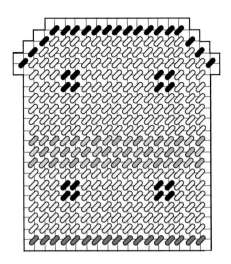

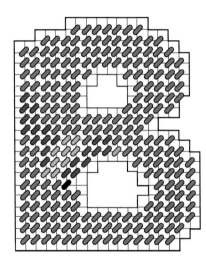

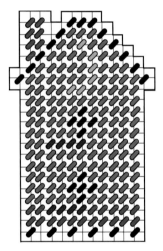

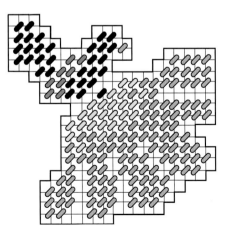

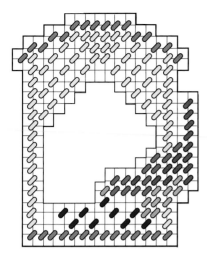
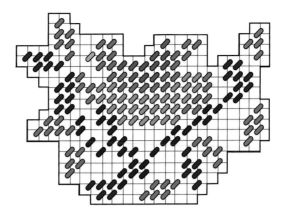
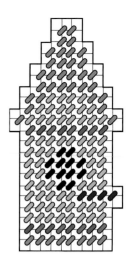
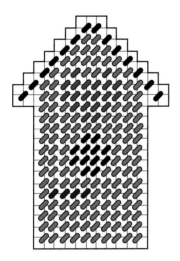
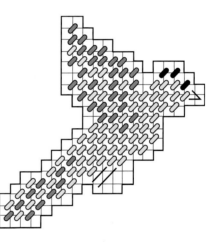
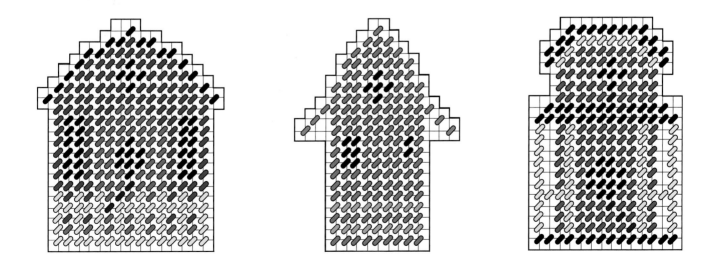

Flower Garden Box

Summer's treasures are intricately executed with garden bunches of dried roses, peonies, and sunflowers divided into geometric patterns and textures.

What You'll Need

3×10×18-inch stained wood shadowbox, with 8 pockets

3 blocks dry floral foam, 3×4×8 inches each

Craft knife

Hot glue gun, glue sticks

22-gauge floral wire

Wire cutters

Sheet moss

7 stems dried pink roses

7 stems dried yellow roses

3 stems dried burgundy peonies

4 stems dried sunflowers

9 stems dried lotus pods (assorted sizes)

2 dried pomegranates

1 stem dried hydrangea

1 package dried linum grass

2 Cover foam lightly with moss around edges, securing with wire pins.

3 Cut dried flowers, fruit, and grass; insert them into pockets in groups. Hot glue if necessary.

4 Cover any exposed foam with moss.

1 Cut and hot glue foam into pockets. Cut wire into 3-inch pieces, and shape pieces into U-shaped pins.

Tips

You can use this same technique on any size shadowbox. The texture box can be used as a table arrangement, or you can hang it on the wall by applying a picture hanger to the back. To add spice and fragrance to your texture box, try using cinnamon sticks, garlic bulbs, or bay leaves.

Decorative Garden Plate

This robin's egg blue display plate is sure to complement your decor—and if blue isn't your color, choose another to enhance your room.

What You'll Need

Clear glass plate

Ruler

Overhead projector pen

Acrylic enamel paint: true gold metallic, baby blue

Fine-line paint bottle with removable metal tip

Waxed paper

Garden theme decoupage papers (or color copy illustrations on page 174)

Scissors

Decoupage finish

1-inch sponge brush

Palette

1 Wash plate. Painting must be done on a clean, oil-free surface.

2 Use ruler and overhead projector pen, on front of plate rim, to make dots every 1½ inches around outside rim of plate. Connect dots by making scalloped lines. Several scallops may need to be adjusted if dots do not come out evenly.

3 Pour gold metallic paint into fine-line bottle. Screw on metal tip. Place plate upside-down on piece of waxed paper. Follow scalloped lines to paint gold lines on back of plate. Paint gold line around inner edge of plate rim and make dots with paint between scallops. Remove metal tip, and paint thicker gold line around outside edge of plate rim. (All painting is done on back of plate.) Allow to dry at least 1 hour. Carefully remove marking lines from front of plate with a damp cloth.

4 Cut out designs. Arrange cutouts as you wish them to appear on plate.

5 Place cutouts in position face-down on back of plate. Pour some decoupage finish onto palette. Picking up 1 cutout at a time, use sponge brush to coat front of paper with decoupage finish. Smooth cutout facedown onto back of plate. Repeat for each cutout, being sure to smooth out bubbles and edges. Allow to dry before continuing.

6 Using sponge brush, apply thin coat of decoupage finish over entire center portion of plate back. When dry and clear, apply another coat of finish. Let dry overnight.

7 Squirt puddle of blue paint onto clean palette. Using sponge brush, paint entire back of plate. When dry (about 1 hour), apply a second coat of paint. It may take several coats to get complete coverage.

Creative Stenciling

Contents

Welcome to the World of Stenciling

*W*hat is stenciling? Stenciling is an age-old technique in which paint is applied to a surface through a cut-out template. Designs can be repeated or used alone to achieve a consistent pattern with a hand-made feel. Modern twists to the traditional craft have opened the door to even greater personal style and artistry. With simple step-by-step techniques that are easy to learn and master, walls and accessories can be transformed to suit your taste and to create harmony in your rooms. Another bonus of stenciling is that you're able to create one-of-a-kind looks without spending a lot of money. There's no limit to what you can do with stencils!

Most stenciling supplies can be found at local craft and hobby stores; check hardware or home improvement stores for tools such as a level or tape measure if these items aren't already in your toolbox. A wide variety of detailed stencils, high-quality brushes, and other accessories can be found in stencil catalogs as well as online.

STENCILS

Stencils are typically made from a stiff plastic called Mylar (a material that's sturdy enough for repeated use and that cleans up easily), though brass, coated paper, and acetate can also be used. Stencils come in two basic types: single overlay and multiple overlay. This simply refers to the number of stencils required to get a complete image.

Single-overlay stencil

A single-overlay stencil is one layer. These designs are usually simple and have spaces, called bridges, between each part of the image. The bridges create shapes that make up the design; without them, you would see just one big shape and no details! Although pictures that are created with a single-overlay stencil will never be completely realistic, these are good stencils for the beginner. They are easy to apply, allowing you to develop a working technique. As your skills advance, you can make

even single-overlay stencils look more complicated by blending colors, freehanding details, and masking off areas to separate colors for a more realistic effect.

Multiple-overlay stencil

Multiple-overlay stencils allow for more realism. One single design is cut on multiple stencil sheets, as the name implies, with different areas on each overlay. Color is added one layer at a time until the image is complete. The size and detail of the image determine how many layers there are to the stencil. The overlays are matched with registration marks.

Registration marks are usually little holes in the corners of the stencil; make a pen or pencil mark through each hole on the first layer, then line the holes up with the marks on subsequent layers.

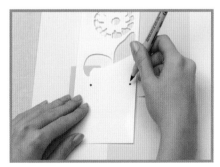

When marking registration points, make a mark through each hole on the first overlay; match up the marks on subsequent overlays.

BRUSHES AND APPLICATORS

Stencil brushes, the most common applicators, have short, stiff bristles of uniform length and come in a variety of sizes. Handles range from straight wood to plastic bulbs; find what's comfortable for you. You will need several brushes, ideally one for each color. This keeps colors from becoming muddy and also speeds things up because you won't have to clean your brush between colors.

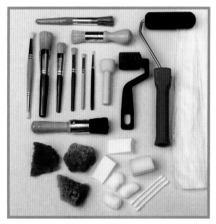

An array of stencil brushes and applicators

Match the brush size to the size of the area to be painted: The brush should be about half the size of the area. This helps contain the paint in the correct areas without having to mask the rest of the stencil. If the whole stencil will be one color, use a bigger brush, which allows you to work more quickly. But if you need to apply a specific color to one tiny area, use a smaller brush to keep the paint where you want it. Use smaller brushes for shadows and highlights.

To obtain different looks, experiment with other applicators. Sponges, which give a less filled-in look, may be cut down to a workable size. Rollers can speed up the project greatly but don't allow for subtle shading or detail. Cotton swabs, cotton balls, cheesecloth, sponges, foam brushes, and spray paint provide unique looks as well.

PAINT

There are two basic kinds of paint used in stenciling: acrylic and oil. Acrylic paint cleans up with soap and water and comes in a wide variety of colors that can be easily mixed to make others. Acrylics dry quickly, so paint doesn't smudge easily. Shading is created by adding other colors on top of the basecoat rather than blending the colors. However, because acrylic paint is very liquid, it is easy to get too much paint on the brush, causing seepage under the stencil.

A variety of paints

TRICK OF THE TRADE *To keep brushes workable while stenciling with acrylic paints, load them with gel blending medium and work them on paper towels to clean and soften.*

Oil paint comes as crèmes and crayons. These take longer to dry, making them ideal for blending and creating smudgy shadows. They're less likely to run under the stencil because of their solid state, but they come in a smaller number of colors. Clean up brushes with mineral spirits or brush cleaner, but dish soap will also work. You need to stencil with oil-base paints on an object that has an oil-paint basecoat.

TRICK OF THE TRADE *Be careful when stenciling, but if you do notice any smudges, touch up work on oil paints with a white art gum eraser.*

ADHESIVE

Adhesive spray or tape holds the stencil in place. Most of the time, tape is the easiest way to adhere a stencil. It's also useful for masking off areas of the stencil you don't want to paint yet. Low-adhesive tape works best, because it adheres well yet won't mar the surface or pull off the paint when it's removed. Keep plenty of low-adhesive tape on hand for every stenciling project.

TRICK OF THE TRADE *Make standard masking or painter's tape a little less sticky by sticking it to your shirt before putting it on the stencil.*

Although spray-on, repositionable adhesives are a little more expensive, messier, and smellier than tape, certain situations call for their use. On a smooth, slick surface, for instance, spray adhesive can be helpful in keeping paint from seeping under the edges of the stencil. Spray adhesive is also ideal for stenciling on tricky or hard-to-reach areas.

TRICK OF THE TRADE *Before using a spray adhesive, make sure your work area is well ventilated.*

PALETTE

When stenciling with oil-based paints, you'll work out of the crème pots they come in. But when working with acrylics, you'll need to place the colors on a palette. Palette paper is sold in craft and art stores for this purpose, but paper or foam plates work just as well. You can also try a piece of matboard or cardboard or even an ice cube tray! Just make sure that whatever you use is big enough to keep the colors separated.

OTHER TOOLS

Depending on the project, there are a few other items that prove indispensable when stenciling. It would be wise to keep all of them on hand.

Art gum eraser. This tool is useful when working with stencil paint crèmes. Because these paints dry slowly, minor smudges and mistakes are easily wiped away with a white art gum eraser.

Artist's brushes. Use these small, thin brushes to add details like shadows or leaf veins.

Index cards. These make handy masking tools for small spaces.

Level. This common tool helps keep a border straight.

Paper towels. Use them to wipe excess paint off brushes, to protect surfaces, and for cleanup. Keep a roll nearby while you're working.

Pencil. Use a pencil for marking level lines and registration marks.

Tape measure. Keep one on hand, or a ruler if you prefer, to determine the amount of space available for the stencil when planning projects.

LET'S PAINT!

With proper preparation and the correct type of paint, almost any surface can be painted. Paint manufacturers are coming out with new formulas all the time, making it easier to carry a decor theme through on almost any item you wish. Here are a few of the different surfaces (other than walls!) you might paint on.

Glass and ceramics. Use paint meant for glass and tile. It comes in transparent colors for a stained-glass look as well as opaque shades. When stenciling glass dishware, paint the bottom of the plate or the outside of glasses rather than the surfaces food will touch. Follow manufacturers' directions for setting the paint.

Fabric. Paints designed for fabric will stay soft and wear better than regular paints. The softness of the paint is less important on items that won't be worn, such as curtains. To stencil on fabric, use spray adhesive on the stencil and tape the fabric down well. Put a piece of cardboard or waxed paper under the fabric to prevent the paint from soaking through. Build up color slowly, as the paint can wick under the stencil if you use too much. Follow manufacturers' directions for heat-setting the paint and washing the fabric.

TRICK OF THE TRADE *If you can't find the color you want in a fabric paint line, add a textile medium to regular acrylic paint.*

Paper. Consider using inks or pigment dyes instead of paint to apply a stencil on paper. These are drier and won't soak into the paper as much. If you must use paint, try painting a basecoat first to stabilize the surface. Then stencil as usual.

Metal. There is a line of paint designed for use on metal without priming, but if you need a color not available in this metal paint, remember to prime the surface first. Otherwise, the paint won't stick.

CHOOSING A DESIGN

Stencils come in many sizes, shapes, and styles. The stencil patterns in this book are just a starting point. Commercially available stencils mimic all kinds of animals, plants, flowers, architectural details, and more. Decide what type of image you're interested in, then look at the style and scale of your options.

Size. The stencil needs to be the right size for the application. A 2-inch-wide stencil wouldn't carry enough weight for a border at the top of a 12-foot wall, but it might be just right to trim a tablecloth. A 20-inch spot motif wouldn't be appropriate for use on a wastebasket, but it can look great stenciled above a window.

Shape. Long, narrow stencils are usually meant as borders rather than center medallions. Many stencils are fluid in their shape: You can rearrange the elements to create a new shape, and thus a new use for the stencil.

Style. The style of the stencil is another checkpoint in choosing a design. This book covers country stenciling, encompassing a wide range of styles from primitive to French to farmhouse. Before you begin, make sure the design you choose works with the style of the room.

PLANNING MAKES PERFECT

It takes more than a little planning to make a stencil look as though it was designed just for your space. The basic rules for planning out your stencil pattern are the same no matter what surface you stencil on.

1. Begin by deciding where you want to stencil. You might want a border in your room, but do you want it at the top of the wall, above the baseboard, or at chair-rail height? Make sure you have a basic idea of what you want the finished product to look like before you continue. It's a good idea to draw your design on a piece of paper first to test different looks.

2. Measure the space where the stencil will go. Then, measure the length of the stencil design, which is called a repeat. How many repeats of the design will fit in the space? To find out, divide the length of the space by the length of the design. For example: The wall is 60 inches wide, the stencil repeat is 12 inches. Five repeats will fit on the wall. You won't always get a whole number telling you how many repeats will fit, however. Most of the time you'll wind up with a fraction of a repeat. While that's not such a big deal in a large wall border, it will stand out on a small project. Be creative in getting the stencil to work in the space: You can stretch or shrink the design by adding or removing space between repeats.

3. Before you begin, do a test to make sure everything will fit. Make samples of your design on a

If a design does not fit a certain space perfectly, repeat parts of the stencil to help fill the space.

piece of paper, and tape them into position. Step back and judge the scale of the stencil for the space. Then check to see how adding or removing space between repeats affects the look of the design. Once you're happy with the design, you're ready to paint!

PROBLEM AREAS

Unfortunately, not every area to be stenciled is a straight, smooth expanse. The space might suddenly become narrower than the stencil, the repeat of the design may fall in a corner, or the surface may be curved, preventing you from stenciling in a straight line.

Ceilings. The ceiling of a room is just like a fifth wall and may be stenciled in the same way. Spray adhesive is a good idea for this surface because without it gravity will cause the center of the stencil to sag down.

Narrowing space. The best way to deal with a narrowing space is to stop the design and restart where the space returns to the normal width. Fill in the narrow space with elements from the original stencil or with a coordinating, but narrower, stencil.

Corners. Both outside and inside corners can be tricky. Even if you try to plan the space so the repeats don't fall in corners, continuous-line stencils, like vines, might have to go through, inside, or around a corner.

For an outside corner, adhere the stencil and work toward the corner, with the excess stencil extending past the corner. Once you've finished with the first side, carefully fold the stencil around the corner, releasing the first side as you tape down the second. Then continue with the rest of the design.

Stenciling an outside corner: Wrap the stencil around the corner, releasing the first side as you tape down the second.

Inside corners are tougher but not impossible. First, mask off the adjoining wall with a strip of vertical tape. Then, much as with outside corners, tape the stencil down and work the first wall, painting into the corner with the rest of the stencil hanging free. Use less paint, a gentle touch, and don't worry if the image doesn't get completely filled in. Then move the stencil to the second wall, leaving the first side loose while you finish stenciling. You can go back later with an artist's brush to fill in details if you like. As long as you don't smear the image or leave globs of paint, admirers will be fooled into thinking the corner is perfect.

For an inside corner, mask off the second wall and let that part of the stencil hang free while you work the first wall.

Curved surface. It's hard to keep a straight line when the stencil won't lay flat on a curved surface. Work the stencil in small sections, readjusting every few inches to keep the image on your guideline. This will provide the illusion of a straight line.

While stenciling is not difficult, it does require knowledge of a few basic techniques. It's a good idea to take the time to practice the techniques before painting on the real surface. This is also the time to test the colors you've chosen and experiment with highlighting or shading.

GETTING READY

The first step in any painting project is to make sure the surface is properly prepared. Generally, this means that it is clean, dry, and in good repair, but some surfaces, such as metal or plastic, may require special preparation. In addition, before you pour that first drop of paint:

• **Mark guidelines to help keep the design level on the wall or the same distance from the edge of the table.** You can't always count on the ceiling or the edge of the stencil to be your guide. They may look straight, but they often aren't! Place a level on the wall to make sure your guidelines are straight, and make a light pencil mark or run a strip of tape to mark the guideline.

• **Pick a starting point.** On a wall, this should be the most inconspicuous place unless you've carefully calculated whole repeats. With accessory projects, you might start on the back of the piece or maybe in the center so the ends come out the same on both sides.

• **Adhere the stencil to the location of the first repeat using either stencil adhesive or tape.** Mark the registration points if you're using a multiple-overlay stencil.

• **If you have a single-overlay stencil with multiple colors, mask off nearby areas you don't plan to paint yet.** Either tape over the open spaces or hold an index card to mask as you paint. This will keep colors from straying.

• **Prepare your palette.** Pour just a small amount of each color, leaving plenty of room between colors so they don't run into each other. If using crème pots, follow the directions on the pots to remove the skin and reveal the paint.

CHOOSING COLORS

Different colors can make a design look entirely different. A dusky rose and Wedgwood blue bring a calm, country feel, while lime green and purple will make it eclectic and funky. Make sure your color choices achieve the effect you're seeking.

LOADING THE BRUSH

Proper loading of paint is crucial to a successful project. Too much paint on the brush causes paint to seep under the stencil, ruining your work. It's always better to start light and build up the color.

To get just the right amount of paint on the brush, dip the flat tip into the paint, then swirl the brush on a paper towel to remove most of it. The brush should feel dry to the touch and shouldn't leave paint if you gently touch your hand to it. If it feels wet, swirl it on the paper towel again to remove more paint.

APPLYING PAINT

There are two basic techniques you can use with a stencil brush. Each gives a slightly different look, and you might find one easier to do than the other.

Stippling. Hold the brush perpendicular to the surface, and tap up and down with the brush to apply color. The effect is that of lots of little dots

To stipple paint, hold the brush perpendicular to the surface and tap up and down repeatedly.

created by the bristles of the brush. With stippling, the stencil is less likely to move around so you're less likely to get paint under the edges. However, when working on a large project, it can get tiring.

To swirl paint, let the brush rest on the surface and swirl it around in a circular motion.

Swirling. This technique is generally used with stencil crèmes, not acrylics. To create a smooth finish, hold the brush perpendicular to the surface, letting it rest just on the surface, and swirl it in small circles to color in the area. Take care not to push the paint under the edges of the stencil. With swirling, there will be some buildup of paint around the edges.

ADDING SHADING

For either of the two methods, when working with just one color, start on

181

Shading with a darker color

the outside edges of the opening and work in to the center. This creates a dark, shadowed edge and light, highlighted center, adding depth to the piece without additional colors. Darken the color by applying more pressure to the brush, not more paint.

When using more than one color, start with the lightest color first to fill in the space and create the highlight. Then use a darker color worked from the outside edge in to the center. You can then dry-brush a darker color to create a shadow effect on the very edges. For realistic shading, a light touch and little paint are needed.

MOVING ON

When you've finished the design, carefully remove the stencil from the surface to avoid smudging any wet paint. Move the stencil over, line it up with your guidelines, and re-adhere to start the next image.

When working with multiple-overlay stencils, it's a good idea to work the entire area with the first overlay, then go back with the next layer, and then the next. This allows the paint to dry before the next stencil goes over it, eliminating the risk of smudges. Acrylic paints, however, often dry quickly enough that it's possible to

complete the entire image at one time before moving on to the next repeat.

OVERLAPPING COMPONENTS

When part of a design seems to "disappear" behind another part, always stencil the object in front first. This keeps ghost images and paint ridges from being visible underneath. After stenciling the first object, cover it with the dropout piece from your stencil and tape in place. This lets you stencil images "behind" the already-stenciled object without worrying about paint drips or overlap ridges.

CLEANING UP

Take some time to step back and admire your artistry, but the work isn't over yet! Proper cleanup will keep your materials in good shape for your next stenciling project.

To preserve the life of brushes and stencils, clean them thoroughly after every use. Acrylic paints clean up with soap and water, whereas oil paints need mineral spirits or brush cleaner. Oil soap, which is formulated for use on wood, is great for cleaning brushes because it won't dry them out. Some plastic stencils just require soaking in water to remove acrylic paint; others need to be scrubbed gently. Try an all-purpose cleaner, using a toothbrush or sponge very gently for any scrubbing. Mineral spirits remove adhesive from the backs of stencils.

TRICK OF THE TRADE *Because the bridges of stencils can be quite delicate, use a soft touch when scrubbing.*

PROTECTING YOUR WORK

While it's not always necessary to seal your work, a clear coat will keep your work fresh for a long time—especially if it's in a high traffic area or if it will be handled frequently. Clear coats range from matte to gloss; decide how shiny you want the surface to be. Keep in mind that the clear coat will change the color and appearance of the surface slightly, so apply it to the entire surface, not just the stenciled area.

TRICK OF THE TRADE *Furniture, floorcloths, and floors need extra protection, so several coats of sealer are necessary on those areas.*

MAKING STENCILS!

We have provided stencil patterns for every project. Enlarge the patterns as indicated, or enlarge or shrink them to fit your space. Once you have the patterns the size you want, it's time to make the stencils.

Almost any kind of clear plastic will make a good stencil because it won't absorb paint and you can see through it to trace the design. The thinner the plastic, the more careful you need to be when cutting out the design, stenciling, and cleaning the template. Buy blank sheets of Mylar at a craft and hobby store, or check the quilting section for large sheets of template plastic. You can also use overhead acetate or X-ray film for making templates.

Another option, though not as durable as plastic, is paper. Cardstock and poster board are rigid and strong enough for accurate stenciling but not flexible enough for bending at corners. You can also treat just about any thick paper with linseed oil to make it waterproof.

DESIGNING THE STENCIL

If you want to make your own design, sketch, trace, or computer-draft the pattern, then use a photocopier to make it the right size.

Decide if this design works best as a single- or multiple-overlay stencil. With a single overlay, you'll have to plan for bridges between major areas of the stencil to make the shapes distinct. For example, a pear would require bridges between the pear and the stem and between the stem and the leaf. The more complicated the image, the more bridges you will need.

Go with multiple overlays for a more realistic finish or if the image is quite detailed. Place a piece of tracing paper over the image, and trace all the parts to be cut out. Then number all the areas for the first overlay with a 1, keeping in mind that images on the same overlay cannot touch each other. Number areas for the next overlay with a 2, and so on until all the areas have been numbered. This tells you how many overlays you will need. Be sure to include dots in the corners for registration points so you will be able to line up the multiple overlays later.

MAKING THE STENCIL

If using a transparent material, lay your design underneath and trace it onto the blank with a permanent marker. Tape the copy and your blank down. For opaque blanks, place carbon paper between the design and

Making a stencil on transparent material

the blank, with the carbon side on the blank and the design on top, then trace the lines. Leave at least an inch of blank material around the outside of the design.

To cut the stencil, you'll need a sharp craft knife or an electric stencil cutter, which makes quick work of cutting plastic blanks. Work on a surface that won't be damaged by the knife or the heat of the cutter; a sheet of glass is ideal.

When making a stencil, cut in one fluid line to achieve a smooth edge.

Try to cut in one continuous line; the piece should just fall out when you're done. If it's still hanging on, take your blade back through the line to get a smooth edge; don't try to pull it, or you'll get a ragged edge. It will take some practice, so don't

be discouraged if your first efforts don't look like a commercial stencil.

Test out your practice designs to see how closely they create the image you want. When you're satisfied, go ahead and start stenciling!

MISCELLANEOUS TIPS

Repair. Stencils sometimes tear, but repairs are easily made. For plastic stencils, you'll need transparent tape and a craft knife. For paper stencils, use masking tape and a craft knife. Tape the top and bottom of the damaged areas, sticky sides together, then cut away the excess tape.

Storage. Stencils should be stored flat. Underbed boxes and dresser drawers are good places for flat storage; you can hang large stencils on pants hangers in a closet. Don't roll or bend a stencil in any way, or it won't lay flat the next time you want to use it.

USING THIS BOOK

The projects in this book include a variety of styles and techniques. Get inspired by the beautiful country colors and designs! You'll find everything from traditional country floral faux wallpaper to romantic French country tiles to a rustic moose lampshade. Each project features complete step-by-step instructions and photos to help make everything easy to understand. Each project is also rated for difficulty and indicates the amount of time needed to complete it. (The time varies based on room size and your experience level.)

Happy stenciling!

Seed-Packet Pots

Enliven ordinary clay pots with these nostalgic
seed-packet designs. Indoors or out, your vegetable
garden never looked so appealing.

WHAT YOU'LL NEED

* Heavyweight paper

* Scissors

* Terra cotta or clay pots, 3

* Delta Ceramcoat acrylic paint:
  White, Ivory, Adobe, Tomato Spice,
  Poppy Orange, Dark Burnt Umber

* Americana acrylic paint:
  Hauser Medium Green,
  Hauser Dark Green

* Accent acrylic paint: Raw Umber

* FolkArt acrylic paint: Bright Pink

* 1-inch stencil brushes, 3

* ⅜-inch stencil brushes, 6

* ⅝-inch stencil brushes, 3

Stencil patterns for this project are located on page 187.

1 Cut a 4×3-inch rectangle out of heavyweight paper. This will be the template for the blank seed packet.

2 Center this paper rectangle vertically on the clay pot, and trace around it with a pencil. Remove the paper. Affix low-adhesive tape around the outer edges of the penciled rectangle, leaving a 4×3-inch open space.

3 Using a 1-inch stencil brush, basecoat the rectangle White. Let dry. Repeat.

4 With the tape still in place, pounce Ivory around the edge of the rectangle with a 1-inch brush. Fade this color into the center, leaving the center area white. Let dry.

5 Stencil each seed packet as follows, using a ⅜-inch brush unless otherwise indicated.

Tomato: Position and tape down the large tomato stencil. Stencil the tomato Adobe with a ⅝-inch brush, concentrating the color on the edges and leaving the center light. Shade around the edges with Tomato Spice. Fill in the lettering with Raw Umber.

Position and tape down the tomato overlay. Stencil the leaves Hauser Medium Green, and shade with Hauser Dark Green.

Carrot: Position and tape down the carrot stencil. Basecoat the carrot Poppy Orange. Shade around the edges with Hauser Dark Green. Stencil the leaf Hauser Dark Green. Stencil the letters Raw Umber.

Position and tape down the carrot overlay. Basecoat the leaves Hauser Medium Green, and shade with Hauser Dark Green. Stencil the carrot's detail lines Hauser Dark Green.

Radish: Position and tape down the radish stencil. Basecoat the radish Bright Pink. Shade around the edges with Tomato Spice, fading into the center and leaving a highlight. Stencil the leaves Hauser Medium Green.

Position and tape down the radish overlay. Stencil the leaf detail Hauser Dark Green and the letters Raw Umber.

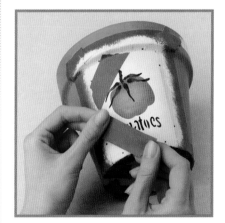

6 At each corner of the seed packet, measure in ⅝ inch both horizontally and vertically along the taped edges. Make a pencil mark on the tape (not on the pot itself) at these measurements. Connect the pencil marks at each corner with a piece of tape placed toward the inside of the seed packet. Stencil these taped-off areas Hauser Medium Green, and add shading around the edges of the triangles with Hauser Dark Green. Let dry, then remove the diagonal pieces of tape.

7 Shade around the edges of the entire seed packet in Dark Burnt Umber with a 1-inch brush. Let dry. Carefully remove the tape from the pot.

8 Center the border stencil vertically on the rim of the pot. Tape in place. Stencil the leaves Hauser Medium Green, and shade with Hauser Dark Green. Use a ⅝-inch brush to stencil the border flowers: On the carrot pot, use Poppy Orange; on the tomato and radish pots, use Tomato Spice. Repeat around the rim.

Seed-Packet Pots

Uncomplicated, simple designs are perfect for sharpening your stenciling skills. Practice on heavy paper first, using multiple colors and shadings to produce more realistic vegetables. Designs like these are especially versatile—try them out on household accessories such as kitchen canisters, backsplash tiles, or pantry doors. However you use them, they'll make quite a statement!

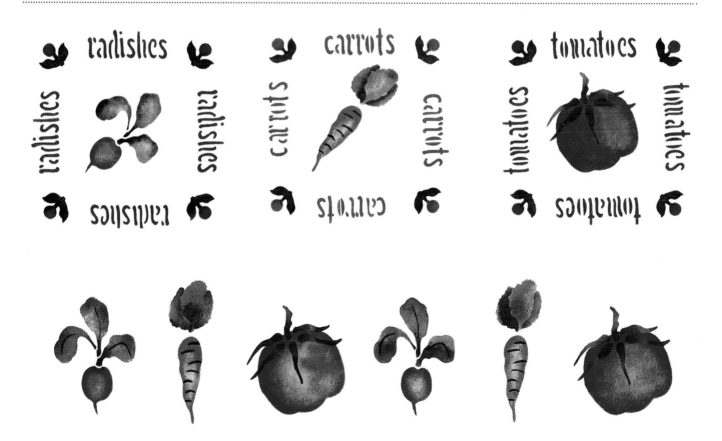

tomatoes

radishes

carrots

A Parade of Keepsake Boxes

Stars and stripes decorate these antiqued keepsake boxes,

creating a special home for treasured mementos.

What You'll Need

✳ 3 papier-mâché boxes: 3-inch star, 4-inch hexagon, 5-inch hexagon

✳ FolkArt acrylic paint: Butter Pecan

✳ Delta Ceramcoat acrylic paint: Blue Velvet

✳ Americana acrylic paint: Antique Maroon

✳ 1-inch foam paintbrushes, 4

✳ ½-inch stencil brushes, 3

✳ 1-inch flat paintbrushes, 3

✳ ¼-inch stencil brush

✳ Antiquing gel

✳ Matte-finish brush-on varnish

Stencil patterns for this project are located on page 191.

3-INCH STAR BOX

1 Basecoat the box Butter Pecan, top of lid Blue Velvet, and sides of lid Antique Maroon with foam brushes. Let dry; repeat.

2 Position the thin stripe stencil along the edge of the lid, and tape in place. With a ½-inch brush, stencil this border Antique Maroon. Repeat the stripe on each of the star's edges.

3 Position the small stars stencils on the lid, and stencil stars Butter Pecan with a ½-inch brush.

4 Load a flat brush with Blue Velvet, and lightly brush the edges of the box and lid.

4-INCH HEXAGON BOX

1 Basecoat the box Blue Velvet, top of lid Butter Pecan, and sides of lid Antique Maroon with foam brushes. Let dry; repeat.

2 Position the thick stripe stencil across the top of the lid, and stencil Blue Velvet with a ½-inch brush. Repeat across lid.

3 Repeat step 2 of the star box to stencil an Antique Maroon border around the lid.

4 Lightly load a flat brush with Butter Pecan, and brush the edges of the box, applying very little pressure. Load a flat brush with Blue Velvet, and lightly brush the edges of the lid.

5 Measuring up 1 inch from bottom, measure and mark the center of each panel of the box from side to side. Working on one panel at a time, position the circular stars/1776 stencil on the mark and tape in place. Stencil with Butter Pecan and the ¼-inch brush. Repeat on each panel.

5-INCH HEXAGON BOX

1 Basecoat the box Antique Maroon, top of lid Antique Maroon, and sides of lid Blue Velvet with foam brushes. Let dry; repeat.

2 Repeat step 2 of the star box to stencil a Blue Velvet border around the lid.

3 Center the large star stencil on the lid, tape in place, and stencil Butter Pecan with a ½-inch brush.

4 Lightly load a flat brush with Butter Pecan, and softly brush the edges of the lid to create a highlight.

5 Measuring up 1½ inches from bottom, measure and mark the center of each panel of the box from side to side. Working on one panel at a time, position the medium-size star on the mark and tape in place. Stencil with Butter Pecan on a ½-inch brush. Repeat on each panel.

6 Load a flat brush with Blue Velvet, and lightly brush the edges of the box and lid.

FINISHING

1 Load a flat brush with antiquing gel, and gently offload the excess on a paper towel. Using a feather stroke and almost no pressure, apply antiquing gel to all the painted pieces. Let dry.

2 Brush on varnish with a foam brush to seal the paint.

A Parade of Keepsake Boxes

Add classic Americana style to your favorite home accessories with stars and stripes in patriotic colors. This motif works well in any room and on practically any surface. Try embellishing a family room fireplace screen, a table runner, or a desktop. Imagine the 1776 circle of stars as an unusual clock face. To enhance the weathered look, keep the palette dark and apply a crackle-finish or antiquing medium.

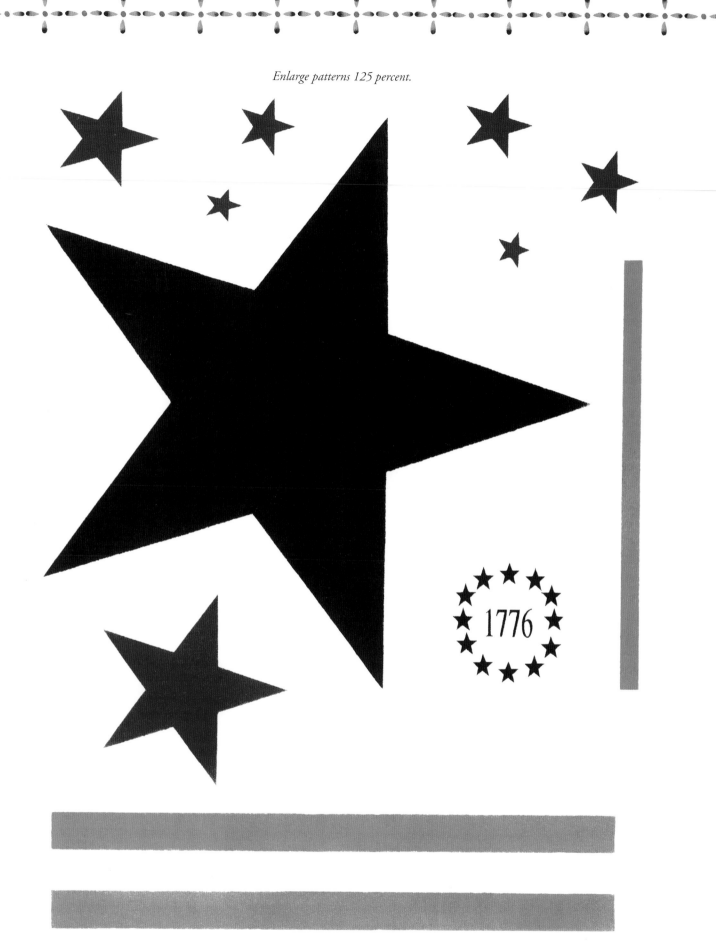

Enlarge patterns 125 percent.

Flowers & Ivy Nook

Winding ivy and sprigs of wildflowers accent this inviting nook,

transforming it into a welcoming, comfortable retreat.

WHAT YOU'LL NEED

* ❋ Scrap paper

* ❋ Scissors

* ❋ Ruler and level

* ❋ Delta Ceramcoat acrylic paint: Wedgwood Green, Dusty Plum, Dusty Purple, Blue Wisp, Avalon Blue

* ❋ Americana acrylic paint: Hauser Dark Green

* ❋ ⅜-inch stencil brush

* ❋ ⅝-inch stencil brushes, 5

Stencil patterns for this project are located on page 195.

1 To prepare the wall, basecoat with latex paint. Before stenciling the flowers onto the wall, first trace all the patterns onto a sheet of paper and photocopy them. Make as many copies as you think you will need (the number of flowers you intend to stencil onto the wall). Cut out each design (you don't have to be too meticulous—a rough outline will do the job). Plan your layout by taping the copies to the wall. Turn the patterns in various directions to avoid a repetitive look, and move them around on the wall until you're happy with the design. Leave at least 6½ inches empty along the bottom for the border.

2 Working on 1 flower at a time, hold each stencil over its paper copy. Tape 1 edge of the stencil in place, and remove the copy. Secure the other edge of the stencil.

3 Unless otherwise noted, use ⅝-inch brushes for all colors. Stencil the designs as follows: **Small Ivy Sprig:** Basecoat the ivy Wedgwood Green, and shade some edges with Hauser Dark Green with the ⅜-inch brush. Also use Hauser Dark Green for the stems.

Five-Petal Flowers: Stencil the leaves Wedgwood Green, and use Hauser Dark Green to shade some of the edges. Stencil the stems Hauser Dark Green. Basecoat 2 of the flowers Dusty Plum, and shade them with Dusty Purple. Base the third flower Blue Wisp, using Avalon Blue for shading.

Small Flower Curl: Stencil the stems and leaves as you did for the Five-Petal Flowers. Basecoat the flowers Blue Wisp, and shade them with Avalon Blue.

4 To create the border, use a pencil and ruler to measure and mark a line 6½ inches up from the floor or molding. Mask the upper edge with low-adhesive tape. Paint this border a shade darker than the rest of the wall. Let dry, and leave the tape in place.

5 Create the border's 2 stripes by placing a strip of tape ¼ inch below the upper edge of the border and another strip ⅜ inch above the molding. Paint the stripes Dusty Purple. Let dry, and remove the tape.

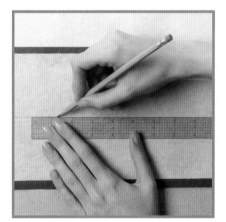

6 Use the ruler and pencil to measure and mark a faint pencil line horizontally through the center of the border. Use the level to check that the line is horizontal. This will provide a guideline for the ivy placement.

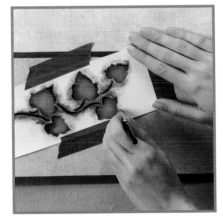

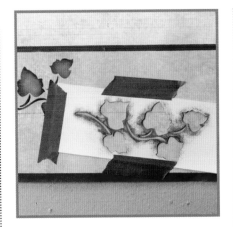

9 Repeat steps 7 and 8 until the border is complete.

TRICK OF THE TRADE *Using paper cutouts to plan the design before painting allows you to fill the space in the best way possible.*

7 Position the stem of ivy stencil A at the beginning of the pencil line, and angle the leaves upward so the top leaf is about ¼ inch from the top stripe. Stencil this ivy as you did the ivy in step 3. Remove the stencil.

8 At the end of stencil A, position ivy stencil B on the pencil line. Angle the leaves down this time, with the bottom leaf in this group about ¼ inch from the bottom stripe. Remove the stencil.

Flowers & Ivy Nook

Design your own custom wallpaper and border with this stencil combination. Or consider this pattern for built-in shelves, a pantry, or a small hallway. For a brighter palette, work the stencils in cheerful spring shades. Extend the charm by stenciling a flower or two onto a mirror, throw pillow, or coordinating floorcloth.

Enlarge patterns 125 percent.

Ivy B

Ivy A

Barnyard Animals Chair

What child wouldn't welcome the opportunity to read

a book or tell a story while perched on this charming

little chair? It's a treasure they'll save forever.

WHAT YOU'LL NEED

* Child-size wood chair

* Sandpaper

* Wood sealer

* Delta Ceramcoat acrylic paint: Light Ivory, Light Foliage Green, Mello Yellow, Crocus Yellow, Tomato Spice, Cape Cod Blue

* Delta stencil paint crème: Garden Green, Cottage Blue, Basic Black, Sunflower Yellow, Yellow Ochre, Warm Brown

* 1-inch flat brushes, 6

* ½-inch stencil brushes, 4

* ¼-inch stencil brushes, 4

* 1-inch foam paintbrush

* Index cards

* Toothpick

* Satin-finish spray varnish

* Satin-finish brush-on varnish

Stencil patterns for this project are located on page 199.

1 Prepare the wood for painting by lightly sanding it with fine-grade sandpaper, applying a wood sealer, and basecoating as follows: Using flat brushes, paint seat, seat apron, and backrest slats Light Ivory; top edges of backrest slats and 1-inch squares on front corners of seat Light Foliage Green; front of vertical rails and 1-inch stripe around seat 1 coat Mello Yellow followed by a thin coat of Crocus Yellow; rungs of legs and ¼-inch stripe on front edge of seat Tomato Spice; and chair legs and sides of vertical rails Cape Cod Blue. Let dry.

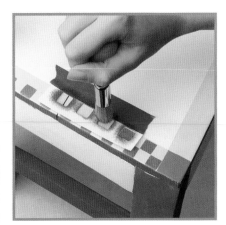

2 To make the seat border, tape the checkerboard stencil to the edge of the seat. Using Tomato Spice and a ½-inch brush, stencil the first row of checks along the edge of the seat. Lift the stencil, and move it 1 row to the right and 1 row in. Be sure the corners of the checks touch. Repeat around the entire seat border, except for the green corner squares.

3 To add a stripe between the checkerboard border and the seat, tape 2 index cards together, ⅛ inch apart. The space between them will be the stripe. Position the stripe so it touches the edge of the checkerboard border. Tape in place, and stencil the stripe Light Foliage Green on a ¼-inch brush. Repeat around the seat so the entire checkerboard is edged in green.

4 Tape the chicken wire stencil to the small backrest slat, and swirl Garden Green into the openings of the stencil on a ¼-inch brush. Move the stencil over, and repeat until the chicken wire covers the backrest slat, front and back. Repeat on the seat apron.

5 Tape the cow stencil onto the seat, and mark the registration points. Basecoat the cow Cottage Blue using a ½-inch brush, and shade with Basic Black on a ¼-inch brush. Stencil the horns, tail hair, and hooves Basic Black. Stencil the bow on the cow's tail Tomato Spice. Remove the stencil.

6 Position the cow overlay, and tape it in place. Stencil the nostrils, eyes, and body markings Basic Black. Let dry.

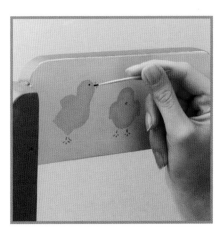

7 Tape chick stencil C to the left corner of the seat. Using a ½-inch brush, stencil the chick Sunflower Yellow. Add shading with Yellow Ochre on a ½-inch brush, and stencil the chick's feet and beak Warm Brown on a ¼-inch brush. Use a toothpick and Basic Black to add a small dot for the chick's eye.

8 Repeat step 7 to stencil chick B in the seat's right corner.

9 Before stenciling the chicks' tracks onto the seat, use a pencil to mark where they will go. Once you're happy with the placement, tape down the stencil and stencil the tracks Basic Black.

10 To stencil the top slat on the backrest, follow the instructions in step 7 to stencil 3 chicks onto the backrest, referring to the photo for placement. Use the face overlay for the middle chick, and stencil the beak Warm Brown and the eyes Basic Black. Mask off the chick on the left, then stencil a checkerboard border around the slat (see step 2). Repeat the design on the back of the slat.

11 Mist the entire surface of the chair with at least 2 coats of spray varnish, letting it dry between coats. Let this dry several days, and then use a foam brush to brush on 2 smooth coats of varnish for more protection from the hands and feet of little ones.

Barnyard Animals Chair

Count your chicks—they're likely to hatch everywhere once you begin this easy design! Change the color of the checkerboard to coordinate with your decor, and stencil a fun wraparound border. Mix and match your favorite barnyard elements to enliven different areas of the playroom for a down-on-the-farm look.

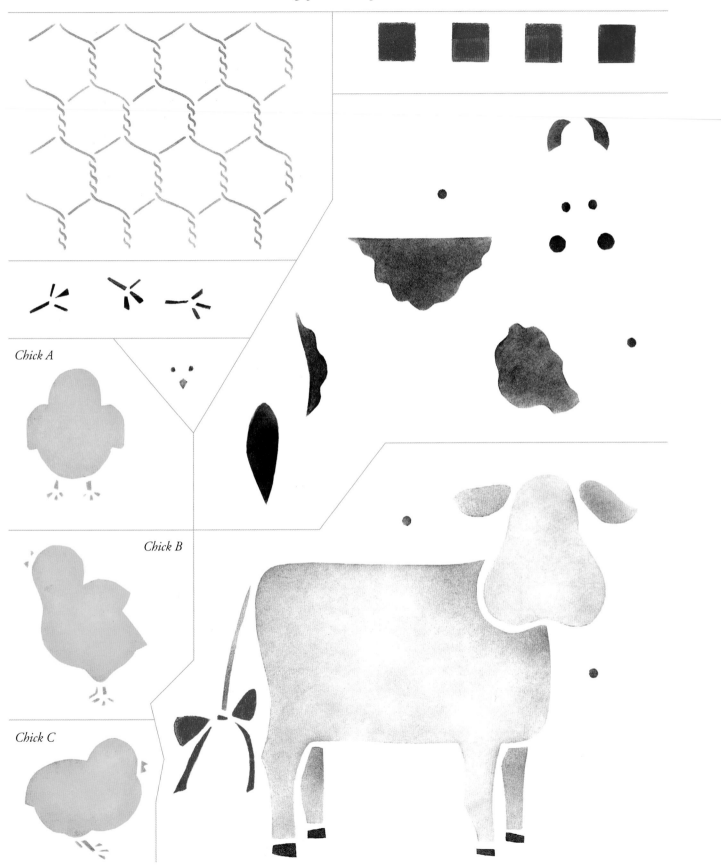

Enlarge patterns 125 percent.

Chick A

Chick B

Chick C

French Country Kitchen

Behind the warmth of a French country kitchen

lies a brilliant surprise . . . the blue tiles, as well as

the dramatic swag, are faux treatments!

WHAT YOU'LL NEED

* Delta Ceramcoat acrylic paint: Periwinkle Blue, White, Light Ivory, Dark Burnt Umber

* FolkArt acrylic paint: Blue Ink

* ⅝-inch stencil brushes, 2

* ⅜-inch stencil brushes, 2

* 1-inch stencil brush

* Heavy paper or cardstock

* Craft knife

Stencil patterns for this project are located on page 203.

FLORAL SWAG

1 Determine where the swag will be painted on the wall, then measure and mark a vertical line where the center will be. Use a plumb line or level to make sure the line is straight.

2 The swag stencil provided is only half the image. Line up the stencil along 1 side of the guideline, and tape it in place.

3 Basecoat the entire stencil in Periwinkle Blue with a ⅝-inch brush, then shade with Blue Ink using a ⅜-inch brush. Let dry.

4 Flip the stencil over and line it up with the first half of the image. Tape the stencil in place, masking your previous work on the center edge. Repeat step 3.

FAUX TILES

1 To create a tile stencil, measure and mark a 4×4-inch square on heavy paper or cardstock, leaving at least 1 inch as a border around all 4 edges. Cut out the square with a craft knife.

2 Position the homemade tile stencil on the wall just above the countertop. Basecoat the tile White with the 1-inch brush, then shade around the tile's edges with Light Ivory on a ⅝-inch brush, brushing in about ½ inch on all

4 sides. Let dry completely, and remove the stencil.

3 Position the floral design stencil on the tile, and tape it in place. Basecoat the design Periwinkle Blue with a ⅝-inch brush, and use a ⅜-inch brush to shade the "insides" of the flowers with Blue Ink (see photo for the detail). Let dry.

4 Reposition and tape down the square tile stencil. For a dimensional effect, lightly shade just the edges of the tile with Dark Burnt Umber using a ⅜-inch brush, shading over the blue flower petals in the corners.

5 Reposition the tile stencil ⅛ inch from the first tile. This will create the illusion of a grout line.

6 Repeat steps 2–5 for each faux tile.

TRICK OF THE TRADE *For an extra-special look, install decorative wood molding to help define your faux tiles. In our photo, we added ¼-inch molding to the top and to the bottom.*

French Country Kitchen

Make this elegant swag the focal point of any room! Add flourishes and flowers to further embellish the design, or subtract any of the elements for a more restrained look. With a simple change of color, you have a brand-new swag. Adding faux tiles is a stylish way to dress up a room. Vary the look by dropping out some of the center designs, using different patterns and colors, or changing the color of the background grout.

Enlarge patterns 125 percent.

203

Garden Butterfly Border

These graceful blue and yellow butterflies inspire

imagination and whimsy in any room of the house.

WHAT YOU'LL NEED

* Delta stencil paint crème:
  Amber, Bark Brown, Colonial
  Green, Paprika, Basic Black,
  Goldenrod, Cottage Blue,
  Garnet Red

* ½-inch stencil brushes, 5

* ¼-inch stencil brushes, 3

*Stencil patterns for this project are
located on page 207.*

1 Use a pencil, ruler, and level or plumb line to indicate where the border will be stenciled. Make sure the lines are parallel to the mirror frame.

2 Center the grapevine stencil on the pencil line, and tape it in place. Stencil the vine Amber using a ½-inch brush, then add Bark Brown shading with a ¼-inch brush anywhere a twig disappears behind another. Repeat all the way around the pencil line.

3 Working in groups of 3, indicate the placement of leaves around the grapevine. Use the 3 different leaf shapes, and vary the placement so as not to create a pattern.

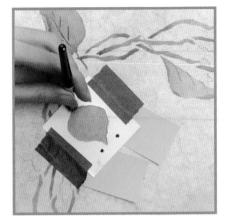

4 Position and adhere the leaf stencils 1 at a time. Mark the registration points. Use a ½-inch brush to stencil the leaves Colonial Green, making them darker at the stem and around the edges. With a ¼-inch brush, add tints of Paprika. Next, use a ¼-inch brush to subtly shade with Basic Black. Let the colors blend gently, and avoid making each leaf exactly alike.

5 For each leaf, align the registration marks of the second overlay, and tape it down. Stencil each leaf detail Colonial Green, and lightly shade with Basic Black.

6 Position the butterflies between the leaves, balancing the blue and yellow. Make a light pencil mark to indicate placement.

7 Adhere the small butterfly stencil to the wall where indicated, and mark the registration points. Stencil this butterfly Goldenrod with a ½-inch brush. Remove the overlay, and wipe clean. Position the second overlay, and stencil the wing detail Amber. Stencil the body and antennae Basic Black. Repeat for all of the small butterflies.

8 For all of the large butterflies, use Cottage Blue and a ½-inch brush on the first overlay. Mark the registration points before removing the stencil. Then position and tape down the second overlay, and stencil all the details Basic Black.

9 Plan where you will stencil the berries. Position and tape down the berries stencils, and apply Garnet Red with a ½-inch brush. Repeat around the vine.

Garden Butterfly Border

This stencil pattern can be interpreted with as much or as little free-form style as you choose. Fashion a unique vine with just the leaves and berries, and accent it with a single butterfly. Bring a rainbow of color into your room with multiple colors of butterflies. On the back of a chair, across a pillowcase, or along the edge of a shower curtain, let your imagination lead the way.

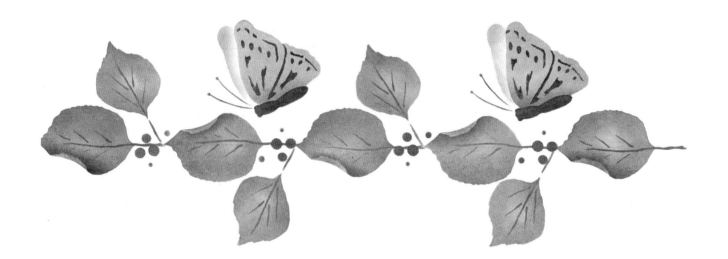

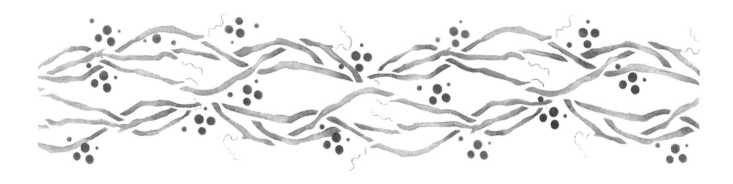

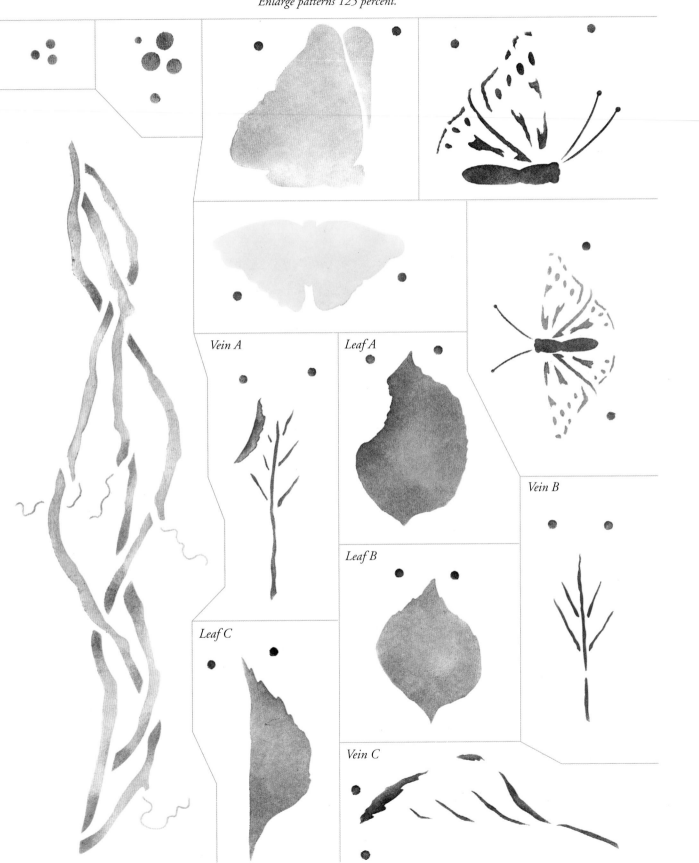

Enlarge patterns 125 percent.

Vein A

Leaf A

Vein B

Leaf B

Leaf C

Vein C

207

Rustic Moose Lampshade

This delightful lampshade brings the charm of a rustic cabin

style home. Its bold, graphic design will light up the room.

WHAT YOU'LL NEED

* Paper lampshade
* Delta Ceramcoat acrylic paint: Brown Iron Oxide
* FolkArt acrylic paint: Licorice
* 1-inch stencil brush
* ½-inch stencil brush
* ⅝-inch stencil brush

Stencil patterns for this project are located on page 211.

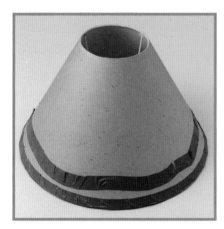

1 To create the "ground" along the bottom edge of the lampshade, apply low-adhesive tape all around the bottom edge. Next, apply another piece of tape above the first one in an irregular, bumpy line, leaving about ¼ to 1 inch of space between the 2 strips as you move around the shade. This will give the illusion of slight hills and valleys across the landscape. Press firmly on the edges of the tape to make a seal so paint does not seep underneath.

2 With the 1-inch brush, apply a solid coat of Brown Iron Oxide to the entire ground area. Use the ½-inch brush to shade the top and bottom edges (along the tape lines) with Licorice. Remove the tape, and let dry.

3 Position the moose stencil so the hooves touch the ground. Tape in place. Stencil with Brown Iron Oxide using the 1-inch brush. Shade the edges of the moose with Licorice, using the ⅝-inch brush.

4 Adhere the moon stencil above the moose. Stencil the moon with Licorice paint using the ⅝-inch brush.

5 Continue the "landscape" by stenciling trees and grass around the shade. Position the stencils along the ground line, and stencil all of the landscaping with Licorice. For visual interest, make the trees different heights by shortening the trunks of some when you place them along the ground line.

TRICK OF THE TRADE *If any parts of the stencil flip up (like the antlers), use your fingers to hold them down while you continue painting.*

Rustic Moose Lampshade

A single moose makes a strong, graphic statement, and the rust and black shades work well with the wrought-iron base, but why stop there? Change your palette to rich greens and browns for a subtle change. Work the moose and landscape elements together to dress up a fireplace screen, window shades, or even the back of a jean jacket. For a simpler project, consider just the trees and grasses as repeat designs on muslin curtains or throw pillows for a family room.

Enlarge patterns 125 percent.

Welcome Friends Hallway

The warm colors and heartfelt

sentiment expressed in the border say it all.

Welcome! We're so glad you're here.

WHAT YOU'LL NEED

* Light Ivory latex wall paint

* Delta Ceramcoat acrylic paint: Blueberry, Antique Gold, Light Ivory, Moroccan Red

* Index cards

* ½-inch stencil brush

* ¼-inch stencil brushes, 3

Stencil patterns for this project are located on page 215.

1 Prepare the wall by basecoating with satin- or eggshell-finish Light Ivory latex wall paint.

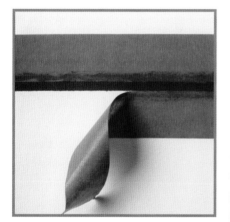

2 The border is created by taping off and painting stripes of varying widths. To begin, measure and make a light pencil mark before placing the tape. Use a level to make sure the lines are parallel to the floor. Locate the bottom of the border, and mask it off with tape. Measure up ⅛ inch, and mask off this stripe. Paint it Blueberry using the ½-inch brush. Let dry, and remove the tape.

3 Measure up ⅛ inch from the Blueberry stripe (this space remains Light Ivory). Mask off another stripe above the Light Ivory stripe, this one ⅝ inch up. Paint it Antique Gold. Let dry, and remove the tape.

4 Again measure up ⅛ inch (another Light Ivory stripe), and mask off a 7-inch stripe for the center band of the border. Paint this band Blueberry, let dry, and remove the tape.

5 Finish off the border stripes by masking and painting as before, but this time in reverse order: ⅛-inch Light Ivory, ⅝-inch Antique Gold, ⅛-inch Light Ivory, and ⅛-inch Blueberry.

6 To stencil the border, center the words "Welcome Friends" in the Blueberry band, and secure with tape. Stencil the letters Light Ivory with a ¼-inch brush. Measure 7 inches from both ends of "Welcome Friends." Reposition the stencil at these points, and paint. Repeat "Welcome Friends" across the entire width of the border.

7 Center the heart motif between the repeats of "Welcome Friends," and tape it in place. Stencil the heart Moroccan Red, the dots Light Ivory, and the leaves Antique Gold using ¼-inch brushes. Repeat across the entire border.

8 Position the dot/leaf design in the Antique Gold stripe. Stencil the dot Moroccan Red and the leaf Blueberry. Repeat across the top and bottom gold stripes.

9 Position the tree 1 inch above the border, centered above the "Welcome Friends" wording, and tape in place. Stencil the tree Antique Gold, the heart and apples Moroccan Red, and the leaves Blueberry. Repeat above every "Welcome Friends" on the border.

10 For a wallpapered look, stencil the heart motifs on the wall at regular intervals: Measure up 13 inches from the top of every heart motif in the border, and position the heart motif there. Stencil the heart Moroccan Red, the dots Antique Gold, and the leaves Blueberry. Measure up 10½ inches from the top of the heart above every tree, and repeat the stencil. To add more rows, measure up the same increment from each heart motif, and repeat. Use a level or plum line to make sure the hearts are aligned.

Welcome Friends Hallway

The variations for this flexible design are endless. Piece together the leaves, the dots, and the hearts in all kinds of different configurations to fit your space. Try stenciling these country icons onto tablecloths, chair backs, pillows, or any other surface that strikes your fancy!

Enlarge patterns 125 percent.

Welcome

Friends

Note: Blue dots above are stenciled
Light Ivory in border.

215

Geranium Window Shade

Add a splash of color to a workaday room with this design.

Whether tumbling across a roller shade or sprucing up a box,

these geraniums will be a perennial favorite.

WHAT YOU'LL NEED

* Window shade

* Delta stencil paint crème: Garnet Red, Garden Green, Basic Black, Christmas Green, Black Cherry

* ½-inch stencil brushes, 2

* ⅜-inch stencil brushes, 3

* Satin-finish spray varnish

Stencil patterns for this project are located on page 219.

1 Draw a soft pencil line about 6 inches from the bottom of the shade, making sure the line is level. Measure and mark the center of this line to determine where to start stenciling.

2 Position the geranium stencil so that the mark you made is in the center of the round blossom marked "center." Tape in place, and mark the registration points. (Note: The stencil provided is only half the image. After stenciling the first half, flip the stencil over and stencil the other half.)

3 Stencil all the flowers Garnet Red with a ½-inch brush, keeping the paint application light.

Then stencil the **leaves** and stems Garden Green on a ½-inch brush. Don't worry if some of the Garnet Red gets on the geranium leaves: This helps to tint the leaves, which adds depth to your painting. You may even tint other parts of the leaves with the Garnet Red brush.

4 Shade the geranium leaves with Basic Black and a ⅜-inch brush. Focus on areas where the leaves emerge from a stem or come from behind another leaf or flower. Remove the stencil, and wipe it clean.

5 Position and tape down the leaf detail overlay. Stencil the detail Christmas Green on a ⅜-inch brush, and shade with a tiny bit of Basic Black. Remove the overlay, and wipe it clean. Let the stencil crèmes dry completely.

6 To execute the second half of the image, flip the geranium stencil over and position the center blossom on top of the already-stenciled center blossom. Do not restencil this flower or the one below it. They are strictly for registration. If you'd like, mask these flowers with an index card. Tape the stencil in place.

7 Repeat steps 3–5 to stencil the second half of the geranium pattern.

8 If you need to stretch the design to fit the width of the shade, mask everything on the geranium stencil except the last 4 leaves. Position these leaves at both ends of the design, adhere, and stencil. Don't forget the leaf detail! When the design is as long as you desire, add more flowers wherever you want using the individual blossom stencil.

9 Use the small petal stencil, a ⅜-inch brush, and Black Cherry paint to define each flower. Stencil these petals (or parts of them) in several places on each blossom, letting the petals extend beyond the edges of the blossom as well.

10 Finish by misting the stenciled area with at least 2 coats of spray varnish, letting it dry between coats.

Geranium Window Shade

These geraniums can be bold and bright or soft and subtle. Work the stencil as much or as little as you like to create a rambling window "garden" or single flower motif. Create stripes of flowers, with or without the leaves, vertically or horizontally. Consider stenciling all or parts of the image on a floormat, picture frame, or towel hems. Brighten up any room in the house with this cheery design.

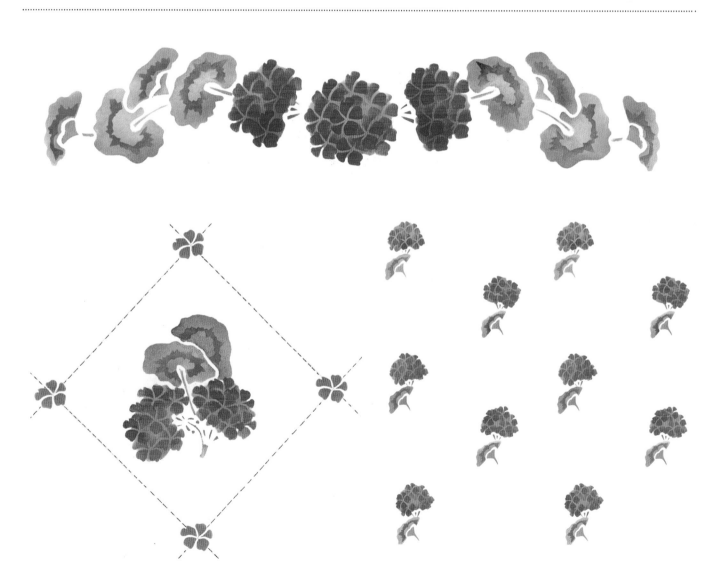

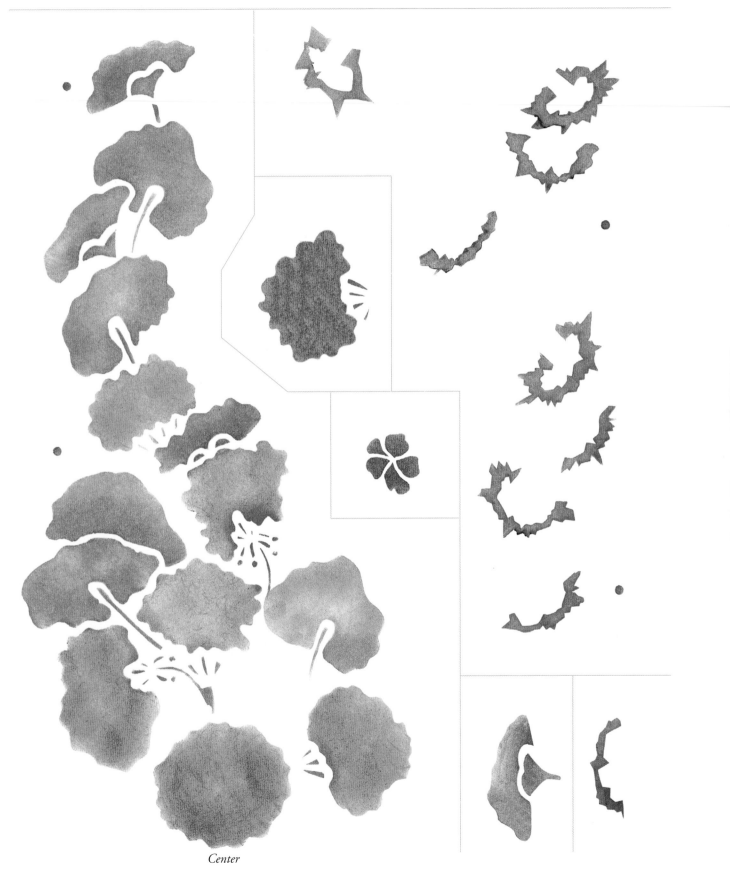

Enlarge patterns 125 percent.

Center

Country Crows Mail Sorter

Classic country elements produce old-fashioned appeal in this easy project. You'll love the charm this country mail sorter delivers to your home.

WHAT YOU'LL NEED

* Unfinished mail sorter
* Delta Ceramcoat acrylic paint:
  Butter Cream, Candy Bar Brown
* FolkArt acrylic paint:
  English Mustard, Licorice
* 1-inch foam paintbrushes, 3
* ½-inch stencil brushes, 2
* ¼-inch stencil brushes, 2
* 1-inch flat paintbrushes, 2
* Antiquing gel
* Matte-finish brush-on varnish

Stencil patterns for this project are located on page 223.

1 Basecoat the mail sorter Butter Cream using a foam brush. Let dry, then paint the bottom, sides, and front panel Candy Bar Brown with a foam brush.

2 Center the "Mail" stencil on the front section of the sorter, and tape the left side in place. Stencil English Mustard with a ½-inch brush.

3 Center the house/crows/star stencil on the back section of the mail sorter, and tape in place. Stencil the house Candy Bar Brown with a ½-inch brush, the chimney and crows Licorice (¼-inch brush), and the stars English Mustard (¼-inch brush).

4 Position the second overlay of the house stencil, tape in place, and stencil the roof, windows, and door Licorice. Stencil the star English Mustard with a ½-inch brush.

5 Place the checkerboard stencil along the top edge of the sorter, tape in place, and stencil Candy Bar Brown with a ½-inch brush. Move the stencil over, and repeat the checkerboard along the entire top edge of the sorter.

6 Using a flat brush and English Mustard, add detail along front edges of the mail sorter using light, feathered strokes.

7 To give the mail sorter an antiqued look, load a flat brush with antiquing gel. Gently offload the excess on a paper towel. Using a feather stroke and almost no pressure, work from the edges into the center to apply the gel. Let dry.

8 Use a foam brush to brush on at least 1 coat of varnish to protect the mail sorter.

221

Country Crows Mail Sorter

Traditional country style lasts through the ages with good reason. The crisp, graphic images look fresh and original whether rendered in dark or bold colors. Choose your favorite folk elements for a set of stacked bandboxes, a recipe box, or kitchen canisters. Create an enchanting country village simply by repeating the house motif in various colors.

Enlarge patterns 125 percent.

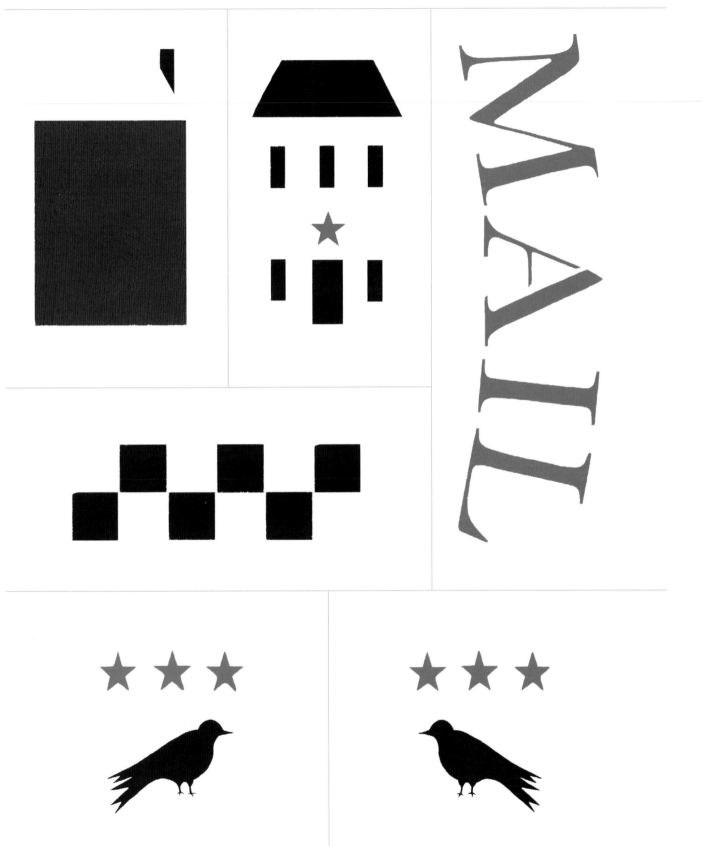

Teddy Bears Border

*Buttons and bears dance on the moon, sending happy dreams
and sweet slumber to your little one.*

WHAT YOU'LL NEED

✲ 4-inch sponge roller

✲ Delta Ceramcoat acrylic paint: Mello Yellow, White

✲ Delta stencil paint crème: Cape Cod Blue, Goldenrod Yellow, Yellow Ochre, Amber, Bark Brown, Garnet Red, True Blue, Garden Green, Basic Black

✲ ¾-inch stencil brush

✲ ½-inch stencil brushes, 3

✲ ¼-inch stencil brushes, 6

✲ Index cards

Stencil patterns for this project are located on page 227.

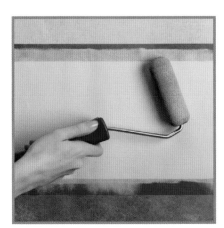

1 Measure and mark a horizontal pencil line on the wall for the top edge of the border. Measure down 7¼ inches from this line, and mark another pencil line to hold the border. Use low-adhesive tape to mask the outside edges of the border. Use the sponge roller to apply an even coat of Mello Yellow to the border. Leave tape in place.

2 Position the diamond stencil on the wall with the top and bottom corners touching each edge of the border and aligned vertically. Tape in place.

3 Rinse roller. Using the sponge roller loaded with White, basecoat the diamond. Continue painting diamonds around the room, repositioning the stencil so the points of each diamond touch.

4 Reposition the stencil on each diamond, and stencil with Cape Cod Blue, using the ¾-inch brush and concentrating on edges.

5 Adhere the moon stencil in the center of the first diamond. Stencil the moon White on a ½-inch brush. Repeat in each diamond.

6 Reposition the moon stencil in the first diamond. Stencil the moon Goldenrod Yellow with a ½-inch brush. Shade the outside edges with Yellow Ochre on a ¼-inch brush. Repeat in each diamond.

7 There are 3 different bear stencils. Position one on each moon, alternating them in whatever order you like. Stencil the bears Amber (except for the ears, feet, and muzzle) using a ½-inch brush, and shade with Bark Brown and a ¼-inch brush. Stencil the ears, feet, and muzzle Bark Brown. Stencil the hanging bears' bows Garnet Red, the

sitting bears' bows True Blue, and the sleeping bears' bows Garden Green on a ¼-inch brush. NOTE: Cover the moon with its dropout to protect it while stenciling the hanging bear's arm. Remove the moon dropout to expose the bear's paw, and mask the rest of the arm with an index card while stenciling the hand. (You may want to cut the index card to fit first.)

8 Position open-eye face overlay on the sitting and hanging bear, and the closed-eye overlay on the sleeping bear, and carefully stencil the eyes, nose, and mouth Basic Black on a ¼-inch brush.

9 Place the button stencil at the point where 2 diamonds meet. Stencil the button White. Reposition

225

and stencil buttons between each diamond. By the time you've stenciled all the buttons, the ones you started with will be dry. Starting at the beginning, reposition the stencil, and stencil the buttons Garnet Red, then shade lightly with Basic Black. Once the buttons are dry, place the overlay detail on top, and stencil with Basic Black.

TRICK OF THE TRADE *Put tape all the way around the stencil to keep it secure while stenciling and to prevent paint from going where it doesn't belong.*

Teddy Bears Border

Decorating a baby's room calls for all sorts of tiny touches. Just add these adorable bears to a chest of drawers, curtains, or cubbies. A simple moon with a cluster of buttons and a colorful ribbon may be all you need to embellish a toy chest or rocking chair. Whether you have a tiny nook or a wide-open wall to decorate, this design provides just the right touch of color and sweetness.

Country Cupboard

Display your collectibles against a picture-perfect backdrop!

Your precious finds sparkle on the stage of this

charming decorative cupboard.

WHAT YOU'LL NEED

✳ Americana acrylic paint: Jade Green

✳ Delta Ceramcoat acrylic paint: Gamal Green, Dark Burnt Umber, Berry Red, Burgundy Rose

✳ ⅝-inch stencil brush

✳ ⅜-inch stencil brushes, 4

Stencil patterns for this project are located on page 231.

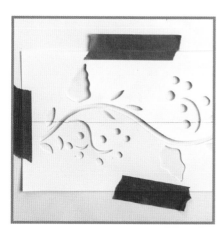

1 Measure and make a light pencil line on the wood behind the shelf. Mark the horizontal center of each stencil as well, and then line up stencil A with the pencil line on the wood. Position and tape down the stencil.

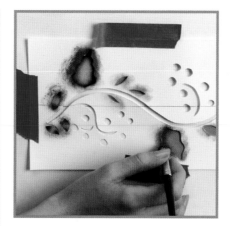

2 Basecoat the leaves Jade Green with the ⅝-inch brush, and shade the leaves with Gamal Green on a ⅜-inch brush. Stencil the berry stems Gamal Green with a ⅜-inch brush. Stencil the vine branch Dark Burnt Umber and the berries Berry Red, also with ⅜-inch brushes. Remove the stencil, and let dry completely.

3 Line up stencil B at the end of stencil A, and repeat step 2. Let dry.

4 Repeat steps 2 and 3 to stencil the vine-and-berry design across the width of the shelf.

5 Repeat steps 1–4 for each shelf area. For contrast, on the middle shelf basecoat the leaves with Burgundy Rose on a ⅜-inch brush and shade them with Dark Burnt Umber. Then paint the berries Jade Green, and use Gamal Green for shading. The vine branch remains Dark Burnt Umber.

TRICK OF THE TRADE *As an alternative, you could also stencil pieces of this design directly onto the wood front of a piece of furniture. Just make sure to protect your finished work with spray varnish.*

Country Cupboard

Add a hint of country loveliness with this winding vine of leaves and delicate berry sprays. Carry the look across the kitchen soffit, around a china saucer, or along a creamy linen tea towel. Change the stencil placement to twist the vine into a wreath or curve over an arched doorway. Alter the colors to suggest a variety of berries.

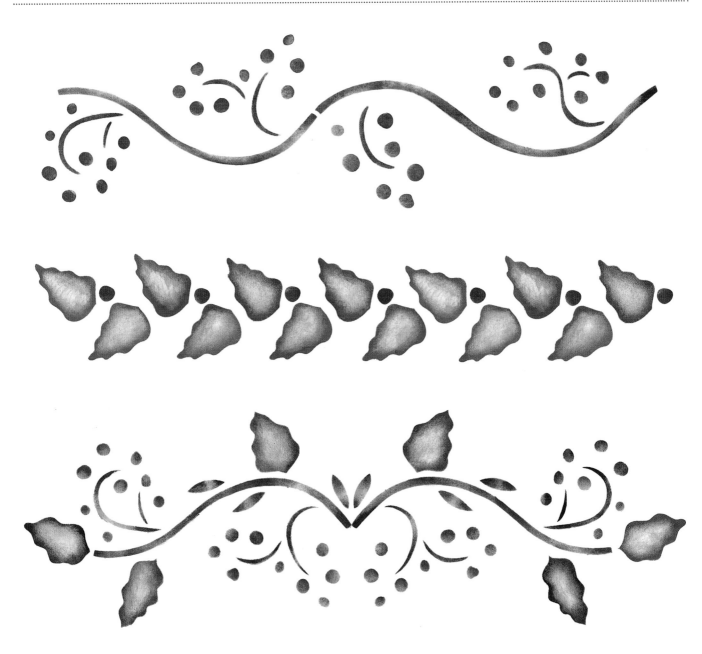

Enlarge patterns 125 percent.

Grapevine A

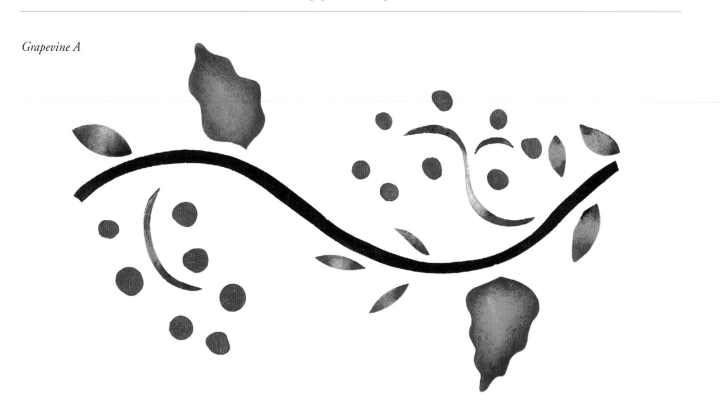

Grapevine B

Sunflower Pillows

Cheery sunflowers and country checks grace these inviting toss pillows. They offer country comfort along with casual elegance.

WHAT YOU'LL NEED

* 12-inch-square cardboard
* Repositionable stencil adhesive
* 11-inch-square prewashed muslin
* Cardstock or heavyweight paper
* Scissors
* Delta stencil paint crème: Sunflower Yellow, Amber, Bark Brown, Garden Green, Jungle Green, Basic Black, Sandstone, Colonial Green
* ⅝-inch stencil brushes, 5
* ⅜-inch stencil brushes, 3
* Disappearing-ink marking pen
* Iron-on adhesive
* Pillow, 12 to 14 inches square
* Brown fine-point permanent marker, optional

Stencil patterns for this project are located on page 235.

1 Mist the cardboard square with repositionable stencil adhesive. Lay the muslin on the cardboard, and smooth it onto the sticky surface so the fabric will not move while stenciling.

2 Before you begin stenciling, you'll need to make a simple shield to protect the sunflower petals while you're stenciling the leaves. To do this, trace or stencil the outline of the sunflower onto a piece of cardstock or heavyweight paper. Lightly stencil the leaves as well, if you wish. Cut out the flower shield, and set it aside.

3 Position and adhere the large sunflower stencil in the center of the muslin square. With a ⅝-inch brush, swirl Sunflower Yellow onto the petals. Stencil the center of the flower Amber with a ⅝-inch brush. Don't worry if some of the Amber gets on the petals; this will provide nice shading. Shade to the lower left and center of the petals with Bark Brown on a ⅜-inch brush.

4 To stencil the leaves, place the flower cutout from step 2 over the stenciled flower petals. Use Garden Green and a ⅝-inch brush to fill in the leaves. Shade with Jungle Green and then very lightly with Basic Black, using a ⅜-inch brush for each color. Remove the stencil and the flower cutout; let dry.

5 Tape the small checkerboard stencil along one edge of the muslin square. Stencil the first row of checks along the edge of the muslin Basic Black, then lift the stencil and move it 1 square over and 1 row up to stencil the inside row of checks. Be sure the corners of the checks touch. Repeat until the checkerboard is stenciled all the way around the muslin.

6 Divide the muslin square into 4 squares of roughly the same size, marking the lines lightly with the marking pen and ruler. (Make sure you don't mark over the stenciled sunflower or the checked border.) Mask the flower and leaves with their dropouts. Mask off the upper left and lower right squares with tape, and stencil the remaining 2 squares Sandstone with a ⅝-inch brush. Let dry.

7 Remove the tape, and mask the Sandstone squares. Stencil the other 2 squares Colonial Green with a ⅝-inch brush, using a light, swirling motion to achieve a textured effect. Let dry.

8 Iron the stenciled muslin square onto a square of iron-on adhesive. Follow the manufacturer's directions to iron the muslin onto the pillow.

233

TRICK OF THE TRADE *To further dress up the pillow, add your own freehand detail. To add lovely script, use a ruler and disappearing marking pen to mark lines 1 or 1½ inches apart in 2 of the squares. With the same pen, write the word "Sunflower" repeatedly on the lines, letting the words "hide" behind the flower petals and leaves. Trace over the words with brown permanent marker.*

We also added faux stitching around the outline of the sunflower and the squares: To make straight lines, simply place a ruler where you want the stitching to be, and, using brown marker, draw a dashed line against it. For curved lines, carefully freehand the dashed lines.

Sunflower Pillows

Who says a sunflower has to be yellow? Change the palette to decorate walls for a teenager who loves candy-colored daisies. Use them to make a swag along the edge of a bed skirt, curtains, or perhaps a bed canopy with stenciled flowers scattered on sheer fabric. Checkerboards of all sizes mix and match with this design, whether creating quilt patterns or connecting the flowers in a border of blooms.

Enlarge patterns 125 percent.

Country Birdhouse Cabinet

Birdhouse lovers (and everyone else!) will flock to this down-home cabinet—a showstopper in any setting.

WHAT YOU'LL NEED

✳ White 2-door cabinet, approximately 18×24 inches

✳ Sandpaper

✳ Wood sealer

✳ Delta stencil paint crème: Garden Green, Basic Black, Dark Barn Red, Amber, Navy Blue

✳ ½-inch stencil brushes, 5

✳ Art gum eraser

✳ Index cards

✳ Matte-finish spray varnish

Stencil patterns for this project are located on page 240.

1 Begin by stenciling the leafy branches, referring to the photo to determine placement. Secure the stencil with tape, and swirl Garden Green on the leaves, varying the intensity of the color. Shade with Basic Black, and tint with a tiny bit of Dark Barn Red. Use Amber on the stems. Reposition until all the branches have been stenciled on the front and sides of the cabinet.

2 Refer to the photo to determine placement of the birdhouses as well. Secure the large birdhouse stencil on the left door of the cabinet, and stencil with Dark Barn Red. Shade around the edges with Basic Black, and apply Basic Black to the roof and the circular opening.

3 To make the post, place 2 pieces of low-adhesive tape about an inch apart directly under the black circle, extending from the birdhouse to the bottom of the cabinet. Stencil the post Amber, making the edges darker than the middle. Add some additional shading with Basic Black under the birdhouse and along the edges.

4 Before you reposition the large birdhouse stencil "behind" the red house, use low-adhesive tape to mask off the top of the red birdhouse. Stencil the second house Navy Blue, and shade around the edges with Basic Black. Also stencil the opening Basic Black. Stencil the roof Amber. Let dry.

5 Hold down the star stencil on the blue house, and erase the paint within the stars with the art gum eraser. Repeat until you're pleased with the star design. (Note: This technique works only with paint crème, not acrylics.)

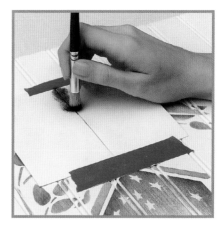

6 "Hang" the blue house from a branch by creating a stripe stencil. Tape 2 index cards ⅛ inch apart. Drag Basic Black over stripe.

7 Tape the small birdhouse stencil to the right of the blue birdhouse, and stencil it Amber. Shade with Basic Black. Stencil the roof Navy Blue and the opening Basic Black. Repeat step 6 to create a "wire."

237

8 Stencil the next small house in the same manner, using Dark Barn Red and Basic Black.

9 Stencil the big birdhouse on the right Amber, and shade with Basic Black. Stencil the roof Navy Blue and the opening Basic Black. While the stencil is still in place, tape down the checkerboard stencil at the top of the birdhouse sides. Stencil the checks Dark Barn Red, then reposition the stencil to paint the second and fourth rows of checks. Be sure the corners of the checks touch. Repeat the checkerboard at the bottom edge of the birdhouse, but stencil only 3 rows of checks here. Repeat step 6 to "hang" this birdhouse from the branch above it.

10 Cover the checkered hanging house with its dropout to protect it, and stencil a small house below it Navy Blue. Shade with Basic Black, and use Dark Barn Red for the roof and Basic Black for the opening. Repeat step 6 to "hang" this birdhouse from the checkered house.

11 To stencil the wren, position the body overlay in the branches at the bottom right of the cabinet, mark the registration points, and stencil with Amber. Add shading with Basic Black. Position the second overlay, and stencil with Basic Black.

12 Mist the entire surface with at least 2 coats of spray varnish. (Let dry between coats.) Then lightly load a brush with Amber and offload on a paper towel. Brush color lightly along the edges of the cabinet. Wipe away excess paint with a paper towel. Apply 2 more coats of spray varnish. Let dry.

TRICK OF THE TRADE *For an antiqued look, before you begin, distress the cabinet by sanding it with a fine- to medium-grade sandpaper, rubbing off some but not all of the paint. Seal with a wood sealer, then basecoat with Antique White. Repeat the process, using Light Ivory this time. Sand one last time.*

Country Birdhouse Cabinet

Bring the outdoors in with your own engaging birdhouse variations. Add them to room dividers, sisal mats, or cupboards to brighten an all-season sunroom. Stretch your design sense, and stencil checkerboards, leaves, and wrens wherever they are inclined to perch. Mix and match for color and style. Antique them to add an aged look. The fun is all yours—the sky's the limit.

239

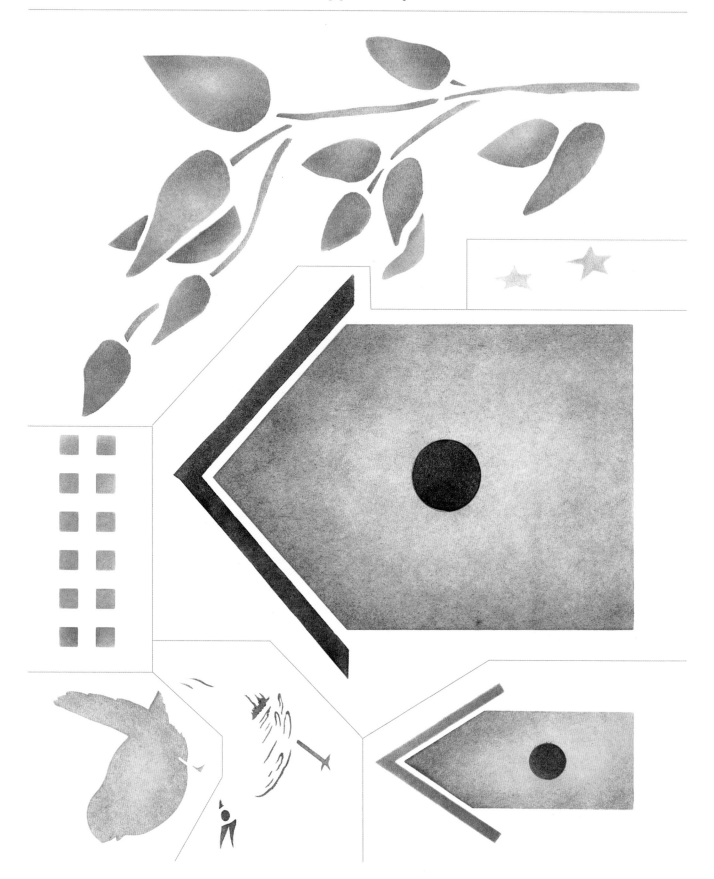

Enlarge patterns 125 percent.

Bountiful Fruit Buckets

Skill Level:
Advanced
Intermediate

Time:
3 hours

Farmstand charm brings these beautiful buckets to life.

What a lovely addition to a kitchen or pantry!

WHAT YOU'LL NEED

* Galvanized metal bucket
* Dishwashing detergent
* Fine-grade sandpaper
* Metal primer
* 1-inch foam paintbrushes, 2
* ½-inch stencil brushes, 6
* Gel blending medium
* Delta Ceramcoat acrylic paint: Apple Green, Tomato Spice, Light Ivory, Calypso Orange, Grape, Medium Foliage Green, Dark Foliage Green, Brown Iron Oxide
* Toothpick
* Satin-finish spray varnish

Stencil patterns for this project are located on page 245.

1 To prepare the bucket, wash it with detergent or a household cleaner. Let dry. Lightly sand the surface with fine-grade sandpaper. Apply an even coat of metal primer with a foam brush, and let dry.

2 With a foam brush, basecoat the bucket Apple Green. Let dry, and repeat.

3 Use spray adhesive to adhere the checkerboard stencil to the top rim of the bucket. Swirl Tomato Spice into the squares, then move the stencil over and repeat the squares all the way around the top. Let dry. Now position the stencil so that the red squares are covered, and stencil the remaining spaces Light Ivory. Repeat to finish the border.

4 Repeat step 3 to create a checkerboard at the bottom of the bucket.

5 Use spray adhesive to adhere the apple stencil to the front of the bucket, centering the bottom of the image between the 2 handles. Basecoat the apple Calypso Orange. Let dry, and then apply Tomato Spice around the perimeter of the apple. The red will be just an outline of color at this point.

6 Before extending red into the center of the apple, flip the dropout of the apple upside down and position it on the bucket so the top curve of the apple covers the section that will become the stem cavity. Hold the dropout in place rather than taping it down. Continue swirling Tomato Spice around the apple and along the bottom edge of the dropout, keeping the center of the apple quite light. Remove the

dropout and work the paint onto the top edge of the apple, leaving a strong Calypso Orange highlight to create the stem cavity. Blend the color along the edges. Let dry.

7 Cover the apple with its dropout to protect it while you stencil the grapes. Basecoat the grapes Calypso Orange. Let dry, then swirl Grape paint onto the entire cluster of grapes. Don't worry at this point about making each grape distinct. Repeat with a second coat of Grape. It's OK if some of the orange shows through.

8 Using the brush that already has Grape on it, pick up a little Light Ivory from your palette. Hold the individual grape stencil in place, and touch highlights onto the right side and around the bottom of each individual grape. Don't strive to make each grape exactly the same; subtle differences and nuances add interest. Using a toothpick, dot Light Ivory highlights on the right side of each grape. Finally, load Medium Foliage Green on the same brush, and lightly add shading between the grapes and the apple.

9 With the apple dropout still in place, position the leaf stencil and basecoat the leaf Calypso Orange. Let dry, then swirl Medium Foliage Green onto the leaf. Shade with Dark Foliage Green near the apple, and add a very thin coat of Tomato Spice over the darkest areas of the leaf. Repeat for the second leaf.

10 Position the pear stencil over the top of the apple dropout, and basecoat the pear Calypso Orange. Let dry, then brush a very soft blush of Tomato Spice, blending it softly into the basecoat. Repeat with Medium Foliage Green to add a tint of green behind the leaves. Remove the apple dropout.

11 Position the stem stencil so it fits into the stem cavity highlight on the apple, and adhere. Stencil the stem Brown Iron Oxide. Flip the stencil over, adhere it to the top of the pear, and repeat.

12 To protect the bucket, spray the surface with at least 2 coats of varnish. Let dry between coats.

TRICK OF THE TRADE *To achieve a realistic three-dimensional effect, apply color more intensely around the edges of the fruit and leaves and keep the centers lighter.*

Bountiful Fruit Buckets

This project is the perfect place to experiment with color and shading. Try a monochromatic color scheme for a subtle look, or turn that Red Delicious apple into a Golden Delicious treat. Perch the apples on a checkerboard rail, or make them the focal point of a tile. Repeat a few clusters of fabulously rich grapes and leaves for a room border, or isolate any element for a canvas market bag. Then sit back, and enjoy the fruits of your labor.

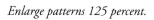

Enlarge patterns 125 percent.

245

Zinnia Garden Border

Skill Level:
Intermediate

Time:
8 hours per wall

Sweet smiles bloom every day in this blissfully

sunny summer garden designed for a princess.

What You'll Need

❋ Light Ivory latex wall paint

❋ 4-inch sponge roller

❋ Delta Ceramcoat acrylic paint:
Mello Yellow

❋ Delta stencil paint crème:
Cottage Blue, Navy Blue, Garden
Green, Basic Black, Goldenrod
Yellow, Amber, Coral, Garnet Red,
Amethyst Purple, Paprika

❋ ½-inch stencil brushes, 6

❋ ¼-inch stencil brushes, 4

*Stencil patterns for this project are
located on page 249.*

1 Basecoat the wall with satin- or
eggshell-finish Light Ivory latex
wall paint.

2 To create 4-inch stripes around
the room, use a plumb line or a
level to extend lines from the ceiling
to the floor at 4-inch intervals around
the room. (Make sure the lines are
4 inches apart at both the ceiling and
the floor.) Mask off both sides of
every other stripe with tape.

TRICK OF THE TRADE *To avoid
painting a wrong stripe, put a small
piece of tape in the stripes you will
not paint.*

3 Use the sponge roller to roll
Mello Yellow onto every other
stripe. Be careful to stay within the
taped area. Let dry.

4 Make as many flowers as you
like around the base of the wall,
stenciling them at different heights
and with different colors. Before you
begin, plan your design and make a
pencil mark to indicate the placement
of each flower, varying flower placement so as not to create a pattern.

5 Each flower has 3 overlays: Work
with the overlay with the largest
open areas first. Position this stencil
on the wall, and tape it to secure.
Mark the registration points. Stencil
each zinnia in the same manner,
referring to the chart on the next

page for color. Apply the basecoat
first, then shade with a darker value.

Petals: Stencil the basecoat darker
toward the center and lighter at the
tips with a ½-inch brush. Swirl on the
darker shading with a ¼-inch brush.

Center: Stencil color with a
½-inch brush, and shade along the
left curve with a ¼-inch brush.

Leaves: Stencil Garden Green with a
½-inch brush, making the color
darker where each leaf emerges from
the stem and along the bottom. Add
a tiny bit of Basic Black shading with
a ¼-inch brush. Apply light tints of
Paprika (½-inch brush) and Garnet
Red (¼-inch brush).

6 Position the second overlay
by matching the registration
points. Tape it down securely, then
stencil the petals as you did in step 5.
Stencil the stem Garden Green,
adding a little Garnet Red at the
point where the flower touches the
stem. If you've positioned the flower
particularly high on the wall, the
stem will not reach the baseboard.
If this is the case, just slide the
stencil down to fill the gap.

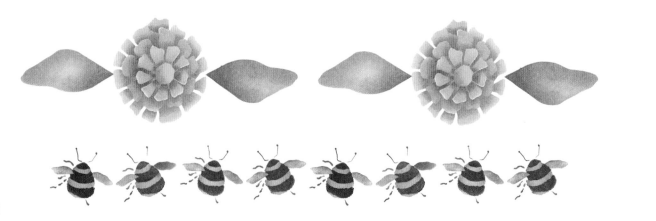

7 Position and tape the third overlay in place, and stencil the petals in the same manner as before. Stencil the vein lines Garden Green, and darken slightly with Garnet Red.

8 Before stenciling the bumble-bees, decide where they will go and make a light pencil mark at each position. Vary their placement throughout the zinnias.

9 Adhere the first overlay (the one without wings) to the wall, and mark the registration points. Stencil with Basic Black.

10 Position and tape down the bumblebee overlay. Stencil the stripes Goldenrod Yellow (½-inch brush) and the wings, legs, and antennae Basic Black (¼-inch brush). Apply paint sparingly to the wings so they look soft and a bit transparent. Shade the edges of the stripes with a small amount of Basic Black on a ¼-inch brush. Repeat steps 9 and 10 for all bumblebees.

TRICK OF THE TRADE *To get the perfect colors for the wall, select your favorite craft paints and take them into a paint store, where you can have latex paint mixed for a perfect match.*

Blue Zinnia
Basecoat: Cottage Blue
Shading: Navy Blue
Center: Goldenrod Yellow
Center shading: Amber

Yellow Zinnia
Basecoat: Goldenrod Yellow
Shading: Amber
Center: Garden Green
Center shading: Garnet Red

Pink Zinnia
Basecoat: Coral
Shading: Garnet Red
Center: Goldenrod Yellow
Center shading: Amber

Purple Zinnia
Basecoat: Amethyst Purple
Shading: Basic Black
Center: Goldenrod Yellow
Center shading: Amber

Green Zinnia
Basecoat: Garden Green
Shading: Basic Black
Center: Coral
Center shading: Garnet Red

Orange Zinnia
Basecoat: Paprika
Shading: Amber
Center: Goldenrod Yellow
Center shading: Amber

Zinnia Garden Border

Get out your paint set, because zinnias come in any color. And since they're the hardy variety, they bloom almost anywhere! Picture them on toy boxes, dresser drawers, or jewelry boxes. Stencil just the petals on pine floors, or make a border of leaves along the edge of the ceiling. Try the bees and little button flowers in smaller places. Create borders and stripes to turn the room into a field of dreams.

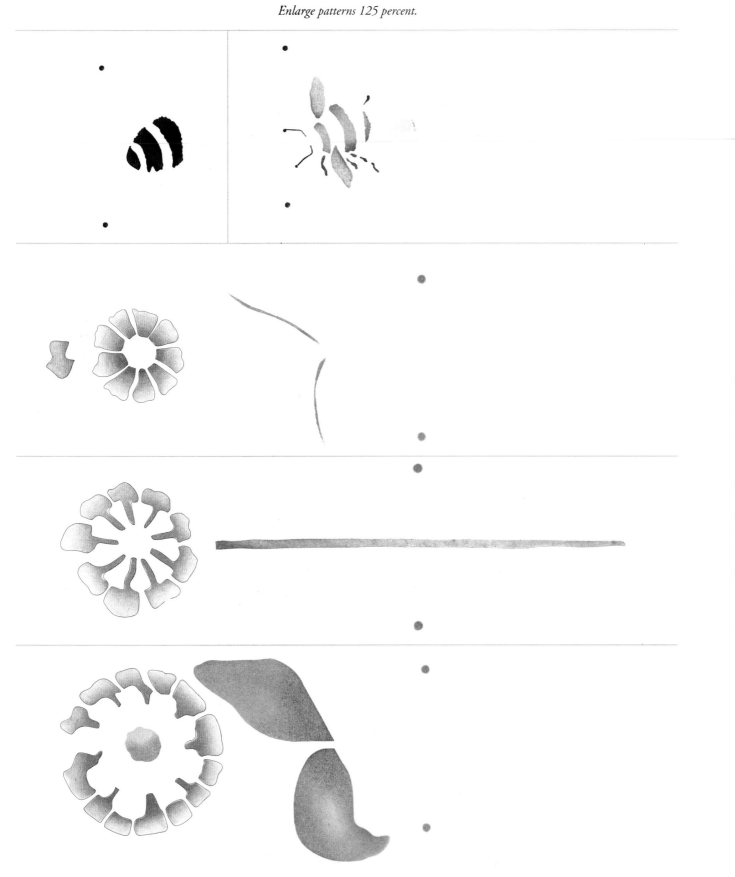

Enlarge patterns 125 percent.

249

Rooster Table Linens

Set your table with country sentiment and vibrant style.

These delightful roosters will give you something

to crow about at every meal!

What You'll Need

* Fabric medium
* Fabric place mat
* Delta Ceramcoat acrylic paint: Maple Sugar Tan, Brown Iron Oxide, Burgundy Rose
* Americana acrylic paint: Hauser Dark Green
* FolkArt acrylic paint: Blue Ink
* ¾-inch stencil brush
* ⅝-inch stencil brushes, 4

Stencil patterns for this project are located on page 253.

1 Follow the manufacturer's instructions to add fabric medium to the acrylic paint.

2 Position the large rooster stencil in the center of the place mat. Tape it in place. Mark the corner registration points on pieces of tape on the mat.

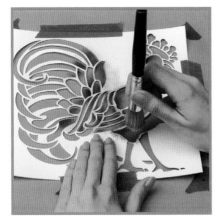

3 Basecoat the rooster's body and the base of the tail feathers (where the feathers attach to the body) Maple Sugar Tan with the ¾-inch brush. Let dry, then shade with Brown Iron Oxide on a ⅝-inch brush.

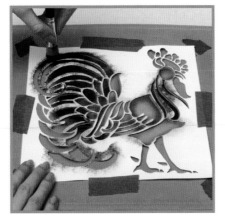

4 Beginning at the base of the tail feathers and working along the length of the feathers, stencil the colors in the following order on ⅝-inch brushes: Brown Iron Oxide, Hauser Dark Green, Blue Ink, and Burgundy Rose. Slightly overlap the colors where they meet each other. Stencil the neck feathers from the head down in the same order, leaving out the Burgundy Rose at the end.

5 Basecoat the rooster's legs, feet, comb, beak, and wattle Burgundy Rose. Remove the first overlay, and let dry.

6 Tape the second overlay in place. Repeat step 4 to stencil the additional neck feathers. Stipple Brown Iron Oxide on the eye and feather detail. Remove the overlay.

7 To stencil the border, line up the stencil along a short edge of the place mat. Tape in place. Stencil the center row of the border Burgundy Rose, letting the paint overlap onto the outer rows of triangles as well. Stencil the outer triangles Blue Ink, slightly blending the 2 colors. Move the stencil along the edge of the place mat, and repeat until the border covers the entire edge. Repeat for the other short edge.

8 Once the short edges are complete, use tape to mask off the corners of the short edges, and repeat step 7 to stencil the border on the long edges of the place mat.

9 When the paint is completely dry, place a soft, clean cloth over the design and run an iron over the cloth to heat-set the paint.

Rooster Table Linens

Center the rooster as a stand-alone design on a chair seat or serving tray. Alter the colors to fit any decorating scheme. Add the geometric border (in any color combination, of course) to backsplash tiles to extend the motif into the rest of the room, or accent candlesticks and napkin rings with a bit of border detail to complete the table scene.

Enlarge patterns 125 percent.

Stencil Resource Directory

Listed below are the names and numbers of the stencils used in this book. Some stencils have been adjusted to fit the size parameters of this book.

The Robins & Willoughby Collection at L.A. Stencilworks

Seed-Packet Pots, page 184
#2241 Mini Stuff
#752 Gardeners' Seed Packets with Holder

Flowers & Ivy Nook, page 192
#609 Mix & Match Stem and Filler Flower Separates
#614 Ivy Separates III

French Country Kitchen, page 200
#2786 Blank Tiles
#3101 Mexican Tile Designs
#216 French Panel Inset

Rustic Moose Lampshade, page 208
#2490 Lodge Vignette II - Moose
#2808 Western Vignette Mini Elements

Country Cupboard, page 228
#3082 Folk Art Kit II

Rooster Table Linens, page 250
#2405 French Rooster
#3075 Folk Art Borders I

Catalogs, stencils, paints, and stenciling supplies are available to order:

L.A. Stencilworks
16115 Vanowen St.
Van Nuys, CA 91406
Toll free: (877) 989-0262
Fax: (818) 989-0405
http://www.lastencil.com
E-mail: lastencil@lastencil.com

Stencils by Nancy

(Please note: Additional stencils are listed below that coordinate nicely with those featured in this book.)

Barnyard Animals Chair, page 196
#LB84c Chicken Wire
#GS51 Checkerboard Stencil
#GS12 Pig, Pig
#GS13 Sheep
#GS15 Pete the Rabbit
#GS16 Liz the Rabbit
#GS37 Toy Truck
#GS79 Tractor

Garden Butterfly Border, page 204
#LB01 Straight Grapevine
#LB44 Three Little Leaves
#GC16 Butterfly Border
#GSG42 Butterfly
#GC07 Creative Grapevine Wreath
#GSG70 Dragon Fly
#GSG55 Bumble Bee

Geranium Window Shade, page 216
#GSG08 Geraniums

Teddy Bears Border, page 224
#GS38 Teddy Bear
#GS39 Sheep Pull Toy
#GS40 Horse Pull Toy
#GS41 Rag Doll
#GS86 Grant the Bear
#GS87 Kaylee the Bunny
#BB02–BB06 Whimsy Moons & Stars

Sunflower Pillows, page 232
#GS51, GS52 Checkerboard
#GSG35 Sunflowers

Country Birdhouse Cabinet, page 236
#GSG13 Two Story Birdhouse
#GS50 Checkerboard
#GSG38 Wren
#GSG22 Leaf Branch
#GSG11 Birdhouse
#GSG10 Cottage Birdhouse
#GSG14 Swingin' Birdhouse

Bountiful Fruit Buckets, page 241
#LB10 Apple
#LB34 Pear
#GSG49 Grapes
#GS51 Checkerboard
#LB83 Lemon
#LB32 Orange
#LB33 Cherries

Zinnia Garden Border, page 246
#GSG41 Zinnia
#GSG55 Bumble Bee

Catalogs and stencils are available to order:

Stencils by Nancy
15219 Stuebner Airline, #28
Houston, TX 77069
Phone: (281) 893-2227
Fax: (281) 893-6733
http://www.stencilsbynancy.net
E-mail: info@stencilsbynancy.net

Primitive Designs

A Parade of Keepsake Boxes, page 188

Welcome Friends Hallway, page 212
(Stencils by Leanne Watson; execution by Nancy Tribolet.)

Country Crows Mail Sorter, page 220

Stencils are sold in sets, but custom orders can be created. Finished items are also available.

Primitive Designs
732 W. Porter Ridge Rd.
Spencer, IN 47460
Phone orders: (800) 803-2620
Questions: (812) 935-7652
Fax: (877) 919-3809
www.primitivestenciling.com
E-mail: questions@primitivedesigns.com

Index

Charming Crafts